simple stitches: Crochet

simple stitches: Crochet

25 PROJECTS
FOR THE NEW STITCHER

CAROL MELDRUM

A Division of Sterling Publishing, Co., Inc.
New York / London

Editor: Amy Corstorphine
Photography: Mark Winwood
Design concept: Beverly Price, www.one2six.com
Production: Laurence Poos
Editorial Direction: Rosemary Wilkinson

10 9 8 7 6 5 4 3 2

First Edition

Published by Lark Books, A Division of
Sterling Publishing Co., Inc.
387 Park Avenue South, New York, NY 10016

First Published in the UK 2010 by
New Holland Publishers (UK) Ltd
London • Cape Town • Sydney • Auckland
Copyright © 2010 text: Carol Meldrum
Copyright © 2010 photographs and illustrations:
New Holland Publishers (UK) Ltd
Copyright © 2010 New Holland Publishers (UK) Ltd

Distributed in Canada by Sterling Publishing,
c/o Canadian Manda Group, 165 Dufferin Street
Toronto, Ontario, Canada M6K 3H6

If you have questions or comments about this book, please contact:
Lark Books
67 Broadway
Asheville, NC 28801
828-253-0467

Manufactured in Singapore

ISBN 13: 978-1-60059-901-9

For information about custom editions, special sales, premium and
corporate purchases, please contact Sterling Special Sales Department
at 800-805-5489 or specialsales@sterlingpub.com.

For information about desk and examination copies available to
college and university professors, requests must be submitted to
academic@larkbooks.com. Our complete policy can be found at
www.larkbooks.com.

contents

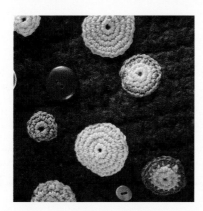

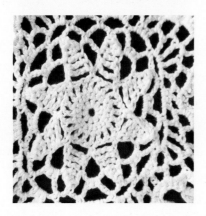

Introduction

The craft of crochet is quite young compared to other needlecrafts such as weaving and knitting. Historically, crochet was used in the mid 19th century to recreate the look of expensive European laces and, during Queen Victoria's reign, it was widely used in clothing and household wares. Today, once again, crochet is as popular as ever for both pleasure and practical purposes. While continuing traditions of the past, we can enjoy delving into tried and tested techniques and dipping into stitches, mixing them up with modern yarns and colors to give crochet a 21st century update.

Crochet is incredibly easy to get started with. Because it involves a repetition of the same movement – drawing the yarn through a loop on the hook – the basics are really quick to pick up. It can feel a little strange to start off with, especially if you are used to knitting, but the fingers soon learn the new movements and the rhythm becomes like a calming second nature. Most of the projects featured are quick to make, often taking only a few evenings to produce. Some larger projects are worked in pieces and are ideal to keep coming back to. You can easily carry your hook and yarn with you wherever you go, making it perfect for filling in those pockets of free time throughout the day. All the essential techniques you need are explained in detail at the beginning of the book, and close-up photos of the projects show the stitch details, making them simple to follow.

Whether you are a complete beginner or already a crochet-pro, by working through the projects you will learn new skills. And, ultimately, what could be better than adding individuality to your outfit with a one-of-a-kind fashion piece or real style to your home!

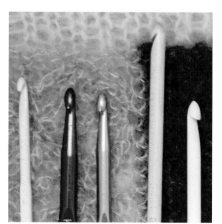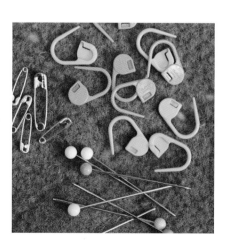

the basics

Tools

You don't need much equipment to get started. The essentials are a hook, some yarn and a pair of sharp scissors. Other equipment can simply be added to your collection along the way.

Hooks There are a wide variety of hooks to choose from and it is a matter of personal choice as to the type of hook you prefer to use. The most commonly used hook is either aluminium or plastic. Smaller steel sizes are used for

working with fine crochet threads and other aluminium hooks have plastic or soft-touch handles to give a better grip, making it a bit easier on the fingers. Bamboo and birchwood hooks have a very smooth finish and often have pretty decorative handles, which add to their appeal.

Hooks also come in a range of sizes from very thin to very thick. It tends to be the rule that thinner hooks are used for finer yarns and thicker hooks are used for thicker yarns, but you can have fun playing about with this once you know what you are doing.

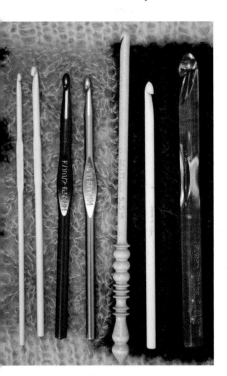

Hooks are sized according to their thickness, either in a number or letter system depending on the brand. The different parts that make up the hook – the point, the throat, the thumb rest and the handle – can vary from brand to brand so try different types to see which one suits you best.

Whichever hook you choose, it's important to look after your tools. It's a good idea to invest in a hook roll with pockets or, alternatively, loops to keep everything in place. Or you could simply use a pencil case or make up bag to keep things tidy.

Pins The glass-headed pin is a good all rounder to have. They are the best type to use when blocking and pressing as plastic and pearl-headed pins can melt with the heat. Quilter's long pins can also be useful when pinning pieces together as they tend not to fall out so easily, but generally I find that you can't go wrong with plain-old safety pins.

Scissors Small pointed scissors are good for cutting and trimming ends and you may find that they also fit snugly in your hook case.

Sewing needles The main type of needle needed is a tapestry or yarn needle, which will have a blunt point and a long eye for threading thicker yarns through. They come in a variety of sizes and are the best type of needle for weaving in ends and sewing up crochet fabrics. You may find that you also need sewing needles with sharp points for certain projects such as appliqué motifs or adding lacy trims to woven fabric.

Stitch markers These are very useful to have in your kit. They are usually brightly colored plastic split rings or shaped loops that easily slip into and around your crochet stitches without splitting the yarn. They are usually used to highlight the beginning of a repeat or indicate the end of a round.

Tape measure Choose one that shows both inches and centimeters on the same side. A 12"/30 cm metal or plastic ruler is also good for measuring your gauge.

Yarns

There are so many different yarns on the market, from shiny mercerised cottons to hairy eyelash yarns, making everything from rough, bumpy textures to smooth, evenly spun strands. In theory you can crochet with any continuous length of fiber, but it is important to understand the fiber content and texture of the yarn as this will affect the finished look and quality of the fabric.

Yarns are created by spinning fibers together. These can be natural fibers, from plants and animals such as wool and cotton, or they can be manmade or synthetic fibers such as nylon or acrylic. Yarns can also be made up of a single fiber or by a blend of different fibers. The various thicknesses of yarns or plies are made up of finer strands twisted together to form the different weights used. Textured and tweedy yarns are often created by twisting several strands of different thicknesses and colors together giving a whole new look. Other yarns are formed slightly differently; ribbon yarns are constructed by knitting a very fine yarn into a tube, giving a rounded or flat appearance on the ball. However, when starting out with crochet it is best to go for a yarn that has a smooth surface and a tight twist.

Generally yarn is purchased by weight rather than length and is packaged in balls, hanks or skeins. The length of the yarn is an important piece of information, especially when you need to substitute one for another, and most brands will give you this information on the ball band. The way in which a yarn is spun can also affect the length. When using hanks or skeins they need to be wound up into balls before they are used to crochet.

Animal fibers Wool is the most commonly used animal fiber and although all wool comes from sheep, there are still a variety of qualities. Merino wool is made from superfine fibers and is very soft and robust, whereas scratchier wools tend to come from sheep that have longer, shaggier coats. Other animal fibers also include mohair and cashmere, which comes from goats, and angora from rabbits and alpacas. Silk is also classed as a natural fiber; it comes from the unwound cocoons of silk worms spun to make a yarn that has a soft shiny lustre. It is also a very strong and light yarn but can be an expensive choice.

Plant fibers Cotton and linen are the most commonly used plant fibers. Cotton really lends itself to crochet and, like wool, it comes in different forms. Different plants produce different types of fibers: cotton can be matte and soft or if you want a bit of a shine, mercerized cotton has a similar appearance to silk. Linen, bamboo and hemp are among the other yarns spun from plant fibers. Linen has a crisp feel and is spun from the fibers of the flax plant. It has a slightly waxy feel on the ball, but drapes beautifully and feels cool to wear. It's also environmentally friendly – as is hemp.

Synthetic fibers Acrylic, nylon and polyester are all made from synthetic fibers. They are processed from coal and petroleum based products, so are essentially the same thing as plastic. Yarns made from 100% synthetic fibers are a lot less expensive, making them a good choice if you are on a budget, but it's best to use one that has at least some natural fiber mixed in if possible. This makes the yarn much nicer to work with and will also give the fabric a more elastic property, helping it to keep its shape.

Getting started

Learning a new skill is great fun, but it is important to understand the basics before starting a project. Work your way through the techniques here, making practice swatches of each of the different stitches. When you come across a new technique in a project, it's a good idea to give it a quick practice first on some spare yarn.

Holding the hook

There are a couple of different methods of holding the hook. There is no right or wrong way but the most important thing is to use the method that's the most comfortable and works best for you. The hook is usually held in the right hand.

Holding the yarn

Again there is no definitive way to hold the yarn, but it should easily feed through your fingers allowing you to create a slight tension that helps keep your stitches nice and even.

Method 1: Hold the hook as if it were a pencil. The tips of your right thumb and forefinger should rest over the flat section of the hook.

Method 1: Loop the short end of the yarn over the left forefinger. The end of the yarn coming from the ball should be under the next finger. Grip the length of yarn towards the ball of yarn gently with your fingers.

Method 2: Hold the hook as if it were a knife, grasping the flat section of the hook between your thumb and forefinger.

Method 2: As before, the short end of the yarn should be over your left forefinger. The end of the yarn coming from the ball should be under your next finger, but then also over the next. Some people also like to wrap the yarn around their little finger in this technique.

Basic stitch techniques

Making the first loop

Every crochet stitch starts and ends with one loop on the hook. All crochet is made up from a series of loops and the first loop begins as a slip knot. Remember, this first loop does not count as an actual stitch.

1 Take the end of yarn in your right hand and wrap around your forefinger on the left hand in a cross. Turn your finger so that the cross is facing downwards.

2 Take the crochet hook in your left hand. Place it under the first loop on your left forefinger and draw through the second loop.

3 Remove your finger and pull both ends of yarn firmly.

Making a foundation chain

The chain is the starting point for nearly all pieces of crochet fabric and is where you work your first row of stitches. The chain is made up connecting loops, and since you need to be able to fit your hook back into the chain, be careful not to make it too tight.

1 Hold your hook in the right hand and yarn in the left. Gently grip the base of the slip knot just under the hook with your thumb and forefinger. This will stop the loop from twirling freely around your hook when you work the chain.

2 Take the hook and place it under the strand of yarn that runs from your hook and over your left hand forefinger. This is described in patterns as yarn round hook, but it is really worked as hook under yarn. Turn the hook with your fingers so the hook part is now facing down. This movement will grab the strand of yarn and allow the hook to move fairly easily back through the loop. Bring the hook back through the loop towards yourself.

3 Slide the loop that you have just made up the shaft of the hook. The neck is much narrower here than the shaft, so if you keep the loop on the neck it will be too tight. Use your right hand forefinger to anchor the stitch and slightly stretch the yarn with your left hand fingers.

Work from steps 2–3 to create the length of chain required for the project. As you work the chain, move your left hand fingers up, keeping them at the base of the chain just worked.

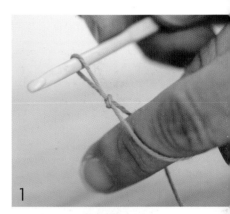

1

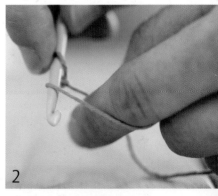

2

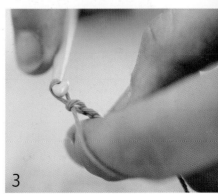

3

Slip stitch (sl st)

The slip stitch is a very useful stitch and is basically a chain that has been connected to the work. Slip stitches are normally used to link a stitch or group of stitches to another point or to move along a row you are working on without having to break off the yarn and rejoin it further along. They are also commonly used when working flat motifs or tubes to join the rows into rounds.

Slip stitches are also used when working a picot. This is when a few chains are joined together at the base of the chain by a slip stitch so that it stands up to create a bobble or picot. The great thing about the slip stitch is that it doesn't add any height to the work so it is perfect for these type of techniques.

COUNTING CHAINS
Each V-shaped loop on the front of the chain counts as one, except the one on the hook, which is a working stitch.

TURNING CHAINS
When working crochet, you need to work a specific number of extra chains at the beginning of a row. These stitches are called turning chains and bring the hook up to the correct height ready for the next stitch to be worked. This ensures the fabric keeps a straight edge. As a rule, the longer the stitch, the longer the turning chain.

Single crochet – 1 turning chain

Half double crochet – 2 turning chains

Double crochet – 3 turning chains

Treble – 4 turning chains

Double treble – 5 turning chains

1 Insert the hook into the stitch. Remember to make sure the hook is under both parts of the stitch.

2 Place yarn round hook and draw through both loops on hook (2 loops on hook) to complete the stitch.

Single crochet (sc)

This is the easiest of crochet fabrics to create. The stitch is good to use in projects that require a compact fabric that you want to be flexible but not too stretchy, like hats and bags. It's also used in basic borders, trims and ties.

Once you have worked the length of chain required, work one extra chain. This is your turning chain.

1 Using the top point of the hook, insert it from front to back into the second chain from the hook. Remember not to count the loop on your hook as a stitch.

2 Using the same method as when making the foundation chain, place the yarn around the hook, then turn the hook so that it faces downwards to catch the yarn.

3 Using the hook, draw the loop back through the chain towards yourself. You should now have 2 loops on the hook.

4 Finish the stitch by placing the yarn round hook again and draw through both loops on hook. You should be left with one loop on your hook. Once you have completed your first stitch, continue along the chain working 1sc (single crochet) into each chain to the end. Start each stitch by inserting your hook into the center of the next chain.

At the end of the row, turn your fabric ready to start a new row. Always work turning stitches at the beginning of each row.

Double crochet (dc)

The double is a longer stitch than the single, which creates a more open fabric. It is used frequently in many open lace fabrics – there are a few variations of the stitch in this book that create slightly different textures, such as in the Sloppy Joe Beret project, which almost looks as if it's been knitted.

The stitch is worked in a similar way to the single except the yarn is wrapped around the hook before working into the fabric. Once you have worked the length of chain required, work three extra chains. This is your turning chain.

1 Before working into the chain, wrap the yarn around the hook as if you were going to work a chain, but do not pull the loop through.

2 Next count 4 chains along from the hook and insert the hook into this chain. The first 3 chains are your turning chain so the place where you insert your hook will be the position of your first stitch. Using the same method as when making a foundation chain, place the yarn around the hook, then turn the hook so it faces downwards to catch the yarn.

3 Using the hook, draw the loop back through the chain towards yourself. You should now have 3 loops on your hook.

4 Next, place the yarn around the hook again and draw through the first 2 loops on hook. You should now have 2 loops on your hook.

5 Finish the stitch by placing the yarn around the hook again and draw through both loops. There is now 1 loop left on the hook and the stitch is complete.

Once you have completed your first stitch, continue along the chain working 1dc (double crochet) into each chain to the end. Start each stitch by wrapping the yarn round the hook before inserting your hook into the center of the next chain.

At the end of the row, turn your fabric ready to start a new row. Always work turning stitches at the beginning of each row.

1

2

3

4

5

Half double crochet and Treble

These stitches are a variation of the double crochet. The half double crochet is slightly shorter than the double crochet and the treble is slightly longer. They can sometimes be used in groups to help create a specific shape, as shown on the earflaps in the Alpine Hat project in this book. They are also used in the White Star Throw, where they help to create the points of the center star and the open lace edge of the larger motif.

Half double crochet (hdc)

The half double crochet is worked in exactly the same way as the double crochet but once you bring the loop through the chain, finish the stitch by bringing the yarn under all three loops at once. Once you have worked the length of chain required, work three extra chains. This is your turning chain.

1 Before working into the chain, wrap the yarn around the hook as if you were going to work a chain, but do not pull the loop through.

2 Count 4 chains along from the hook and insert the hook into this chain. The first 3 chains are your turning chain so the place where you insert your hook will be the position of your first stitch.

3 Using the same method as when working the chain, place the yarn round the hook, then turn the hook so it faces downwards to catch the yarn. Draw the loop you've just made back through the chain towards yourself, leaving 3 loops on the hook.

4 Finish the stitch by placing the yarn round hook again and draw through both loops on the hook. You should be left with 1 loop on your hook.

Once you have completed your first stitch, continue along the chain working 1hdc (half double crochet) into each chain to the end. Start each stitch by wrapping the yarn round the hook before inserting your hook into the center of the next chain.

At the end of the row, turn your fabric ready to start a new row. Always work turning stitches at the beginning of each row.

Treble (tr)

The treble is worked in the same way as the double crochet but the yarn is wrapped around the hook twice before inserting into the fabric.

Once you have worked the length of chain required, work 4 extra chains. This is your turning chain.

1 Before working into the chain, wrap the yarn around the hook twice, as if you were going to work a chain. Count 5 chains along from the hook and insert the hook into this chain. The first 4 chains are your turning chain and the place where you put your hook is the position of your first stitch.

2 Using the same method as when working the chain, place the yarn round the hook, then turn the hook so it faces down the way to catch the yarn. Draw the loop back through the chain towards yourself, leaving 4 loops on your hook.

3 Next, place the yarn round hook again and draw through the first 2 loops on hook. There should now be 3 loops on the hook. Repeat, and you will have 2 loops left on your hook.

4 Complete the stitch off by placing the yarn round hook again and draw through both loops, leaving 1 loop on your hook.

Once you have completed your first stitch, continue along the chain working 1tr (treble) into each chain to the end. Start each stitch by wrapping the yarn round the hook twice before inserting your hook into the center of the next chain.

At the end of the row, turn your fabric ready to start new row. Always work turning stitches at the beginning of each row.

Working in the round

Some crochet projects are worked in rounds rather than in rows. This means that you crochet around the work rather than working back and forth in rows, changing from front to back each time.

Making a ring

This is the first step in working in the round. The ring is usually made up of a small amount of chains with the ends joined together with a slip stitch to form the ring.

1 6ch, insert the hook from front to back into the first chain made.

2 Wrap the yarn around the hook and draw back through the chain and the loop on your hook. Gently tighten by pulling the loose end of yarn.

Increasing in the round

To keep a circular piece of crochet flat, you have to increase evenly around the outer edge of your work; the amount of stitches you increase by each round will depend on the amount worked in the first round. For example, if you worked 10 stitches into the ring then you will increase by a multiple of 10 each time. On the 1st round you increase into every stitch, on the 2nd round you increase on every 2nd stitch, and so on.

Each round should end on an increase. If you don't end on an increase, stop and have a look at your work to find out where the mistake has happened before ripping it out. Finding out where you went wrong will give you a better understanding of how everything fits together.

Working into the ring

The ring forms the center of your work, and by working into the ring you form the first round. When working into the ring, watch that you don't work back over the first stitches, especially when the pattern asks for a large amount of stitches and the ring isn't very big. Depending on the stitch you will be working, make the appropriate length of turning chain. This example is worked in double crochet, so 1 extra chain has been used.

1 Insert the hook from front to back through the center of the ring. With the yarn around hook, pull back and draw through 2 loops.

2 Once you have worked the correct amount of stitches, complete the round by joining the ends together. Simply work a slip stitch into the top of the turning chain at the beginning of the round you have just finished.

Remember that when working in the round, the same side should be facing you throughout.

It's a good idea to use a stitch marker at the beginning of each round as this will help you keep track of where the round stops and starts. Place the stitch marker into the turning chain and move it up each round as you go.

Longer stitches

There are also longer stitches that are an extension of the basic double crochet. They are worked in the same way, but the yarn is wrapped around the hook 3, 4 or 5 times before inserting into the fabric. Each stitch is completed by drawing the yarn under 2 loops at a time until you are left with 1 loop on the hook.

Double treble (dtr) Work 5 turning chains

1 Wrap the yarn around the hook 3 times, then insert the hook into the 6th space from the hook. Place yarn round hook, then draw the loop through towards yourself, leaving 5 loops on the hook.

2 Place the yarn round hook and draw through 2 loops on hook. You should now have 4 loops on your hook. Repeat, leaving 3 loops left on your hook. Repeat twice more, leaving one loop left on your hook.

3 Yarn round hook 3 times. Insert hook into next space and repeat from step 2.

At the end of the row, turn your fabric ready to start a new row. Always work turning stitches at the beginning of each row.

Triple treble (tr tr): Work 6 turning chains and wrap yarn round hook 4 times.
Quadruple treble (qt {or quint} tr): Work 7 turning chains and wrap the yarn round hook 5 times.

Front- and back-post double crochets

This technique is used to create a texture by either pushing a stitch forwards or backwards. It can be used on any stitch but works best on stitches with a visible stem the length of a double and upwards. The front and back post technique is used to great effect in the Sloppy Joe Beret and Hooded Scarf projects.

Front post double crochets (fdc) Wrap yarn round hook and insert hook from the back of work right to left around the **front** of the stem (post) of the stitch, yarn round hook and draw the hook back towards yourself. Complete double crochet as normal – yarn round hook and under 2 loops, yarn round hook and under 2 loops.

You should find that the top of the stitch where you would normally place your hook has been pushed to the front of the work and the V is lying horizontally facing you.

Back-post double crochets (bdc) Wrap the yarn round hook and insert hook from the front of work right to left around the **back** of the stem (post) of the stitch, yarn round hook, draw the hook back towards yourself. Complete double crochet as normal – yarn round hook and under 2 loops, yarn round hook and under 2 loops.

You should find that the top of the stitch where you would normally place your hook as been pushed to the back of the work and the stem (post) of the stitch just worked is raised.

Shaping techniques

Basically shaping is about adding stitches in and taking them away to create a desired shape. The techniques used are the same for working in rows and for working in the round. A basic beret worked from the top down starts by using the increasing technique until you get to the required width, then moves onto the decreasing techniques to reduce the amount of stitches and bring the shape in to fit the head. When working a flat piece of work in rows, increases and decreases are usually worked at the beginning and end of a row. When working in the round, increasing and decreasing techniques are usually worked in even sections around the outer edge of the work.

Increasing

Internal increases This is the most straight-forward method of adding stitches. Simply work 2 or more stitches into the same place. This method, when used in rows, is usually worked 1 or 2 stitches in from the edge. So on a row you would work 1 stitch and then work your increase, work along the row until you had 2 or 3 stitches left, work your increase in the next stitch, and then work 1 stitch in to each until the end.

External increases This method is used to add several stitches at one time. You do this by adding extra chains at the beginning or end of a row. To add stitches to the beginning of a row using this method, work the required amount of chain at the end of the previous row, remembering to add the turning chains. On the next row, work the extra stitches along the chain and continue working to the end of the row.

To add stitches at the end of a row with this method work until the last few stitches. Remove the hook and join a length of yarn to the last stitch on the row and work the required amount of chain. Fasten off the yarn. Place the hook back into the stitch and continue to work to the end of the row and across the extra chains.

Adding stitches in this way this gives your work a much neater finish. The increasing marks become a feature of the fabric and it can also make it easier to sew up.

Decreasing

Internal decreases As with internal increasing, it is best to work this technique at least 1 stitch in from the edge.

Skip a stitch

The easiest and most straight forward way to decrease stitches is to simply skip a stitch from the previous row. This is fine when working in single crochet as it is a tight fabric so missing 1 stitch won't show up, but with longer stitches this method can leave a hole.

Working stitches together

With this method you can work 2 or more stitches together and it is used frequently when working more open fabrics.

To work 2 stitches together, start by working the 1st stitch of the decrease as you would normally but do not complete the stitch. Leave the last loop from the stitch on the hook (there should be 2 loops on the hook). Work the next stitch from the decrease and, again, do not complete the stitch. Leave the last loop on the hook (3 loops on the hook). If you are working more than 2 together, work every stitch in the decrease as above. Complete the decrease by placing yarn round hook and drawing through all the loops on the hook.

External decreases This method of decreasing is used if you want to decrease a few stitches at the same time. It gives the edges a more angular and stepped effect, so works better for certain projects.

To work this decrease at the beginning of a row, work a slip stitch into each of the stitches you want to decrease, then work your turning chain and continue along the row. To decrease at the end of a row, simply leave the stitches you want to decrease unworked, turn and continue back along the row.

Understanding gauge

Gauge in both crochet and knitting is the amount of stitches and rows it takes to cover a certain area, usually a 4" (10 cm) square. However, gauge can vary from person to person even when the same hook and yarn is used as everybody has their own personal gauge. Patterns are written with a specific gauge in mind, so if your gauge differs from the one given, the finished project will turn out either too big or too small.

Making a gauge swatch

Always use the recommended hook size and yarn as given in the pattern. Make a piece of crochet between 4" (10 cm) to 6" (15 cm) square, making sure you work in the same stitch as given in the pattern for the gauge.

1 Fasten off the yarn and block and press the piece gently. Lay the sample swatch on a flat surface with the right side facing you. If you are unsure which is the right side, the tail of the chain should be on the left.

2 Place a ruler or tape measure horizontally across the work and, making sure the ruler is straight, use the stitches as a guide. Place pins into the fabric exactly 4" (10 cm) apart, then count the number of stitches. Include half stitches when counting. Repeat the process vertically to count the rows.

If you are working a stitch pattern, the gauge may be given over the pattern repeat rather than the number of stitches and rows. Work the swatch in the pattern but count the number of pattern repeats between the rows.

Adjusting your gauge

Often people don't realise just how important getting the gauge right is. The whole design is based around these numbers, so if you are out even by a little bit you can end up with a project that is too big or too small. It even affects the amount of yarn needed to complete the project so is well worth taking the time to check your gauge before you start to avoid any disasters.

Tip If the number of stitches and rows in your swatch matches the pattern, you are ready to start. If you find you have too many stitches or rows, your gauge is too tight. Re-do the swatch using a larger sized hook. If you don't have enough stitches, your gauge is too loose. Re-do the swatch using a smaller sized hook.

Getting the gauge correct for both stitches and rows is equally important, but if you can get the right amount of stitches and the rows are slightly out, you can always add rows in or take rows out. The other alternative is to have another look at the size you want to make the finished piece and alter it according to your gauge.

Following the instructions

Finishing techniques

You can spend all the time in the world getting the stitches and shape correct, but if the finish doesn't look good it can really spoil the look of the finished product. It's exciting when you get to this stage, but try not to rush it.

Fastening off

Once you have completed your last stitch, you need to secure the yarn to stop it from all unravelling. This is called fastening off or, sometimes, binding off. Cut the yarn leaving approx 4–6" (10–15 cm) yarn. Draw the loose end through the last loop on the hook and pull tightly to secure.

Sewing in loose ends

Before blocking and pressing a project it's best to sew in all the loose ends. You will need to use a tapestry needle, which has a large eye and a rounded end. Thread the needle and weave the ends in by running it through the stitches nearest to the loose ends. It's easiest to do this with the work inside-out, otherwise the outer seams can look bulky.

Blocking and pressing

Before sewing up, you need to make sure all the pieces are the correct size and shape. To block a piece of crochet, pin the pieces onto a padded surface. An ironing board will do for smaller pieces but you may need to improvise for larger pieces – a wooden board with a few layers of quilters padding covered with a check patterned fabric tea towel is ideal. The check pattern helps you to keep the edges straight and the fabric itself will protect the surface from the iron.

Always check the ball band for care instructions. If it has a high synthetic fiber content do not go near it with the iron as it will go out of shape or, at worst, will melt with the heat. Pin the pieces right side down on the padded surface using glass headed pins. Ease the crochet into shape, then check its measurements against the pattern. For natural fibers place a damp towel over the work and gently hover the iron over at a steam setting. For synthetic fibers or yarns with a high synthetic content, spray the fabric lightly with water. Do not go near it with a dry or a steam iron as the heat will make the fabric loose its shape. Allow to dry before removing the pins.

Understanding patterns

When you first look at a crochet pattern it can look a bit like a foreign language, so it's best to start off with a simple one and build up to something more complicated. It's also good to get into the habit of checking you have the correct amount of stitches at the end of each row or round, and to work through the instructions exactly as they are given. Some patterns can be in chart form as well as written form.

Following the pattern

Most patterns are written as repeats, which are indicated in brackets and with asterisks. It is very important to pay attention to these, along with the commas and full stops. You will also find that the correct amount of stitches, if there have been any increases or decreases in the row, are shown in closed brackets.

Tip All patterns give you information about the project at the beginning. It will tell you what materials you will need, as well as what the finished size will be and any pattern abbreviations. It's important to read through these carefully before you start as they may include a variation of a technique that is important to that specific design.

Seams

There are a few methods of sewing your crochet together, depending on the type of seam you want and the type of project you are making. Pieces can be joined together either by sewing with a large blunt needle, or by using a crochet hook. Generally it is a matter of personal preference, whereby you use the method that you are most comfortable with and gives you the best finish, but sometimes a pattern will ask for a specific type of seam.

Joining stitches at the sides

When joining the front and back of a project together, you can join them almost invisibly together.
- Lay the two crochet pieces side by side and pin together with safety pins. Start by matching up the top and bottom and then the center points. You'll find that even though you have worked the same amount of rows for each piece, there is still slight difference in the length. By pinning the pieces together in this way however, you can easily absorb any slight differences.
- Thread the sewing needle with a length of yarn. Try to use the same yarn that the project has been worked in, or if it's not suitable, go for a yarn that blends into the fabric well. Bring the needle up from back to front, starting from the bottom right hand stitch on the left hand piece, and pull the needle through leaving a 4–6 in (10–15 cm) tail.
- Next place the needle from back to front, starting from the bottom left hand stitch on the right hand piece, pulling

the yarn through and drawing the two pieces of fabric together. Repeat the process once more. Work into the bottom stitches creating a figure of eight and pulling the yarn tight as you go. The yarn will now be secure and you should have an even, straight edge.

The process for working up the side seam differs slightly according to the stitch used for the fabric. For single crochet (sc), you should zigzag between the tops of the stitches. For double crochet (dc), zigzag between the top, middle and bottom of the stitches.
- Bring the needle up through the post of the 1st st on the left hand side, and then do the same for the opposite side. Zigzagging back and forth, insert the needle into the same place you came out of but move directly up one stitch each time. You will sometimes be joining stitches to turning chains but don't worry too much about where about your needle is coming out of — just try to keep everything even.
- After you have worked 3 or 4 rows, gently pull on the yarn to draw the two seams together. They should link up evenly and be more-or-less flat. When you reach the top, secure the yarn by working a few times through the top stitches and weave in the loose end before trimming.

Joining tops together

The way you join the tops of two crochet pieces together is similar to the method for joining the sides. Lay the pieces next to one another and pin together. This time however, instead of working into the stitches or turning chains, you will be joining the tops of the stitches together.
- With the right sides of the fabric facing you, secure the yarn at the beginning of the seam using the figure of eight method as described before. Start by inserting your needle into the bottom most outer loop on the left hand side, then cross over to the bottom most loop on the right hand side. Pull firmly and repeat.
- Work along the rest of the seam. Insert your needle from back to front, coming up through the center of the first V on the left hand side. Move the needle across to the right hand side and insert the needle into the place that the yarn came out from the last figure of eight loop. Pull the needle out through the center of the next V on the same side and zigzag back and forth like this until you reach the end of the seam. Secure the yarn by working a final figure of eight loop.

Joining tops to sides

Joining the top of one piece to the side of another piece uses a combination of the two methods. Stitches are often longer than they are wide, so don't always match up with each other exactly. As you will be working through either the stem of a stitch or the center of a turning chain, it is especially important to pin pieces together when joining tops to sides.

Backstitch

Certain projects need a sturdy non-stretch seam, which is more about functionality than beauty. For projects such as cushions or the base of a bag for example, backstitch is perfect. To join two pieces together using backstitch, have the right sides facing to the inside and pin together, making sure the rows and stitches match up evenly.
- Secure the yarn to the right hand side of the seam by working a few small stitches on top of one another through both layers of the fabric. Insert the needle back into the fabric at the beginning of the seam and draw through to the wrong side. Move the needle up a centimeter or so along the back of the work and bring the needle back through to the right side, pulling the yarn tight. *Next insert the needle back into the end of the last stitch worked and move up the seam a centimeter or so and bring the needle through to the right side, pulling tight. Keep repeating from the * to the end of the seam. Secure the end by working a few stitches on top of one another.

- If you are working a single crochet seam, place yarn round hook and draw through.* Insert your hook into the next stitch through both pieces of fabric, yarn round hook and draw back through (2 loops on hook), yarn round hook again and draw through both loops repeat from * until seam is complete. Break off yarn leaving approx 4–6 in (10–15 cm) length, lace loose end round hook and pull through to secure.

Crocheting seams together

Seams can also be crocheted together. It is very straight forward and easy to do, but does leave a visible seam and is rather bulky so do take this into consideration.
- Place your pieces together either with right sides or wrong sides facing depending on if you want the seam to be on the inside or outside of your work. Pin together making sure that the stitches and rows match up and the ends meet. Next insert your hook through both pieces of fabric on the right hand side at the very outer edge. Make a slip knot, pop it on your hook and draw the hook back through towards yourself. If you are working a slip stitch seam,* insert your hook into the next stitch through both pieces of fabric, yarn round hook and draw back through (2 loops on hook). Draw the first loop under the second loop and repeat from * until seam is complete. Break off yarn leaving approx 4–6 in (10–15 cm) length, lace the loose end round the hook and pull through to secure.

the projects

narrow stripe beret

This beautifully soft beret is a good project to tackle once you are confident with the basic stitches. It is worked in the round throughout so there are no seams to sew up. Make this hat and think of trips to the seaside, lots of fresh air and fish 'n chips!

star rating
★ (beginner)

finished size
Circumference around band 22"/56 cm

materials
- **Yarn:** Rowan Baby Alpaca, DK weight, (approx 109 yd/100 m per 1.75 oz/ 50 g ball)
  A – Jacob, sh. 205 x 2 (Ecru)
  B – Lagoon, sh. 210 x 1 (Pale blue)
  C – Zinc, sh. 204 x 1 (Mid blue)
- **Hook:** G/6 (4.00 mm)

gauge
Using G/6 (4.00 mm) hook approx 20 sts and 19 rows over 4"/10 cm of single crochet

abbreviations
Sc2tog – single crochet 2 together
See also page 125

Using G/4 (4.00 mm) hook and yarn A work 5ch, sl st into 1st ch to make a ring.

Round 1: 1ch, PM (place marker), work 10sc into ring, sl st into 1ch at beg of round. (10 sts)

Move place marker and put after 1ch worked at the beginning of each round.

Round 2: 1ch, work 2sc into the back loop of 1st sc, * 2sc into back loop of next sc, rep from * to end, sl st into 1ch at beg of round. (20 sts)
Change to yarn B – Place yarn B over hook and pull through loop already on hook. Pull yarn A tight so loop disappears into work.

Work into back loop of every sc throughout.

Round 3: 1ch, work 1sc into 1st sc, 2sc into next sc, * 1sc into next sc, 2sc into next sc, rep from * to end, sl st into 1ch at beg of round. (30 sts)
Change to yarn A – As described above.
Round 4: 1ch, work 1sc into 1st and every foll st to end, sl st into 1ch at beg of round. (30 sts)
Change to yarn C.
Round 5: 1ch, work 1sc into 1st 2sc, 2sc into next sc, * 1sc into next 2sc, 2sc into next sc, rep from * to end, sl st into 1ch at beg of round. (40 sts)
Change to yarn A.
Round 6: 1ch, work 1sc into 1st and every foll st to end, sl st into 1ch at beg of round. (40 sts)
Change to yarn B.
Round 7: 1ch, work 1sc into 1st 3sc, 2sc into next sc, * 1sc into next 3sc, 2sc into next sc, rep from * to end, sl st into 1ch at beg of round. (50 sts)
Change to yarn A.
Round 8: 1ch, work 1sc into 1st and every foll st to end, sl st into 1ch at beg of round. (50 sts)
Change to yarn C.
Round 9: 1ch, work 1sc into 1st 4sc, 2sc into next sc, * 1sc into next 4sc, 2sc into next sc, rep from * to end, sl st into 1ch at beg of round. (60 sts)
Keep stripe sequence correct throughout as set from rounds 6–9.
Keep shaping sequence correct by adding 1 onto the amount of sc worked before increasing (working 2sts into same stitch) on next and every 2nd row until there are 140 sts (12 sts between increasing).

Before starting decrease, gently block and press top of beret.

Round 26–28: 1ch, work 1sc into 1st and every foll st to end, sl st into 1ch at beg of round. (140 sts)
Round 29: 1ch, * 1sc into next 12sc, sc2tog, rep from * to end. (130 sts)
Round 30: 1ch, work 1sc into 1st and every foll st to end, sl st into 1ch at beg of round. (130 sts)
Round 31: 1ch, *1sc into next 11sc, sc2tog, rep from * to end. (120 sts)
Round 32: 1ch, work 1sc into 1st and every foll st to end, sl st into 1ch at beg of round. (120 sts)
Round 33: 1ch, *1sc into next 10sts, sc2tog, rep from * to end. (110 sts)
Round 34: 1ch, work 1sc into 1st and every foll st to end, sl st into 1ch at beg of round. (110 sts)
Round 35: 1ch, *1sc into next 9sc, sc2tog, rep from * to end. (100 sts)
Round 36: 1ch, work 1sc into 1st and every foll st to end, sl st into 1ch at beg of round. (100 sts)
Round 37: 1ch, *1sc into next 8sc, sc2tog, rep from * to end. (90 sts)
Round 38: 1ch, work 1sc into 1st and every foll st to end, sl st into 1ch at beg of round. (90 sts)
Round 39: 1ch, *1sc into next 7sc, sc2tog, rep from * to end. (80 sts)
Round 40: 1ch, work 1sc into 1st and every foll st to end, sl st into 1ch at beg of round. (80 sts)
Round 41: 1ch, *1sc into next 6sc, sc2tog, rep from * to end. (70 sts)
Work 7 rounds in yarn A and 1 round in yarn C as row 40.
Break off yarn and fasten off.

to finish

Sew in loose ends to inside of hat.

broad tie belt

This broad tie belt was designed with a touch of 1950's beatnik chic in mind. It is created using the basic stitches but worked to give the fabric a woven textured effect. The denim yarn will fade and change over time, but that just adds to the character. The belt is designed to wrap around the waist and can easily be lengthened to fit any size.

star rating
★ ☆ ☆ (beginner)

finished size
To fit: Average adult waist. After washing, belt measures approx 6"/15 cm wide by 37½"/95 cm long.

materials
- **Yarn:** Rowan Denim, DK weight, 100% cotton (approx 102 yd/93 m per 1.75 oz/50 g ball) Nashville, sh. 225 x 5 (Dark indigo)
- **Hooks:** D/3 (3.00 mm) and G/6 (4.00 mm)

gauge
Using G/6 (4.00 mm) hook approx 20 sts and 20 rows over 4"/10 cm of single crochet

abbreviations
See page 125

Using G/6 (4.00 mm) hook make 30ch.

Row 1: 1ch, 1sc into 2nd ch from hook, 1sc into each ch to end, turn. (30 sts)

Row 2(WS): 1ch, 1sc into front loop of 1st sc, 1sc into front loop of each sc to end, turn.

Row 3(RS): 1ch, 1sc into back loop of 1st sc, 1sc into back loop of each sc to end, turn.

Repeat last 2 rows 6 more times and row 2 once more.

Making holes for the ties

Row 17: 1ch, 1sc into next 4 sts,* 2ch, skip 2 sts, 1sc into next 2 sts, rep from * 5 times more, 1sc into last 2 sts, turn.

Row 18: 1ch, 1sc into next 4 sts, *1sc into each of next 2 ch, 1sc into next 2 sts, rep from * 5 times more, 1sc into last 2 sts, turn.

Ending with WS row repeat rows 2–3 until work measures approximately 35½"/90 cm.

Break off yarn and fasten off.

Outer edge trim

With RS facing and D/3 (3.00 mm) hook, rejoin yarn into sc at top RHS of belt.

Crochet along the long edge using slip stitch, working approx 1sl st into outer edge of each row.

Break off yarn and fasten off. Repeat for other side.

Belt ties

You need to make 12 of these. Using G/6 (4.00 mm) hook make 2ch.

Row 1: Insert hook into 1st loop made, yo and draw through, yo and draw through both loops, 1ch, turn.

Row 2: Insert hook from right to left into small loop at left hand side, yo and draw through loop, yo and draw through both loops, 1ch, turn.

Repeat the last row 138 times.

Break off yarn and fasten off.

to finish

Sew in all loose ends for both belt and ties. Place in a net bag or old pillow case and wash in machine at approximately 60 degrees. Also put in some spare yarn for sewing ties onto main belt. This will get rid of excess indigo dye.

Let the pieces dry and block and press gently into shape.

Using washed spare yarn, sew ties onto main belt, position the ties to match up with the holes.

crochet project bag

This design is perfect for carrying your crochet project around with you when you are on the move. It's practical and pretty with plenty of pockets to keep all your things neatly together. The handles are large enough to fit comfortably over your shoulder and are worked lengthwise so won't stretch.

star rating
★ ★ ★ (beginner)

finished size
Actual measurements: width 13"/33 cm; depth 14"/36 cm

materials
- **Yarn:** Rowan Summer Tweed, 70% silk, 30% cotton (approx 118 yd/108 m per 1.75 oz/50 g ball)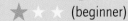
  A – Hedgerow, sh. 550 x 2 (dark green)
  B – Jardine, sh. 544 x 2 (mid green)
  C – Rush, sh. 507 x 1 (light green)
  D – Harbour, sh. 549 x 1 (aqua)
  E – Summer Berry, sh. 537 x 1 (red)
- **Hook:** G/6 (4.00 mm) hook

gauge
Using G/6 (4.00 mm) hook approx 15sts and 16.5 rows over 4"/10 cm of single crochet

abbreviations
See page 125

Base
Using G/6 (4.00 mm) hook and yarn A make 15ch.
Row 1: 1ch, 1sc into 2nd ch from hook, 1sc into each ch to end, turn. (15 sts)
Row 2: 1ch, 1sc into each sc to end, turn.
Repeat row 2, 32 more times.
Break off yarn and fasten off.

Side panel (make 2)
Using G/6 (4.00 mm) hook and yarn A make 15ch.
Row 1: 1ch, 1sc into 2nd ch from hook, 1sc into each ch to end, turn. (15 sts)
Row 2: 1ch, 1sc into each sc to end, turn.
Repeat row 2, 41 more times
Break off yarn and fasten off.

Front and Back panel (Make 2)
Using G/6 (4.00 mm) hook and yarn B make 32ch.
Row 1: 1ch, 1sc into 2nd ch from hook, 1sc into each ch to end, turn. (32 sts)
Row 2: 1ch, 1sc into each sc to end, turn.
Repeat row 2, 41 more times.
Break off yarn and fasten off.

Side pocket
Using G/6 (4.00 mm) hook and yarn A make 13ch.
Row 1: 1ch, 1sc into 2nd ch from hook, 1sc into each ch to end, turn. (13 sts)
Row 2: 1ch, 1sc into each sc to end, turn.
Repeat row 2, 38 more times.
Break off yarn and fasten off.

Large front pocket
Using G/6 (4.00 mm) hook and yarn C make 32ch.
Row 1: 1ch, 1sc into 2nd ch from hook, 1sc into each ch to end, turn. (32 sts)
Row 2: 1ch, 1sc into each sc to end, turn.
Repeat row 2, 28 more times.
Break off yarn C and join in yarn E.
Work 4 rows in sc.
Break off yarn and fasten off.

Medium front pocket
Using G/6 (4.00 mm) hook and yarn D make 32ch.
Row 1: 1ch, 1sc into 2nd ch from hook, 1sc into each ch to end, turn. (32 sts)
Row 2: 1ch, 1sc into each sc to end, turn.
Repeat row 2, 18 more times.

Break off yarn D and join in yarn E.
Work 4 rows in sc.
Break off yarn and fasten off.

Handles (make 2)
Using G/6 (4mm) hook and yarn E make 80ch
Row 1: 1ch, 1sc into 2nd ch from hook, 1sc into each ch to end, turn. (80 sts)
Row 2: 1ch, 1sc into each sc to end, turn.
Repeat row 2, 3 more times
Break off yarn and fasten off.

to finish

Sew in all loose ends.
Block and press all panels, pockets and handles.
Pin and stitch side panels to base.
Pin and stitch back panel to base and sides.
Pin and stitch medium pocket to large pocket, leaving top open, using picture as guide, with yarn E sew medium pocket to large pocket using backstitch approx 3"/8 cm in from edge to create small pocket.
Sew pockets to front panel, then sew front panel to sides and base.
Pin and stitch side pocket to right hand side panel.

Once all panels are stitched together, work top border as follows in the round:
With R.S facing and using G/6 (4.00 mm) hook and yarn E, rejoin yarn to top right hand corner of front panel.
Round 1: 1ch, 1sc into same sc, 30sc across front panel, 14sc across 1st side panel, 31sc across back panel, 14sc across 2nd side panel, sl st into 1ch at beg of round. (90 sts)
Round 2: 1ch, 1sc into 1st st, 1sc into each sc to end, sl st into 1ch at beg of round.
Repeat last row 6 more times.
Break off yarn and fasten off.
Place handles using backstitch, pin and stitch each end of handles to front and back of bag, approx 3"/8 cm in from outer edge and 2"/5 cm down from top edge.

extra long fingerless gloves

These gloves are perfect for keeping your hands and wrists nice and cozy. The extra long cuff fits snugly up the arm and the button detail adds a splash of interest. Being fingerless, they're also very practical as you can still wiggle your fingers and pick things up easily when you need to. Worked in a space-dyed chunky yarn, they crochet up quickly and make a great last-minute gift.

star rating
★ ★ ★ (beginner)

finished size
Actual measurements: width 4½"/11 cm; length 13½"/34 cm

materials
- **Yarn:** Patons Shadow Tweed, 58% wool, 40% acrylic, 4% viscose (approx 145 yd/133 m per 3.5 oz/100 g ball) 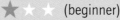 Red/burgundy/orange mix, sh. 6906 x 2
- **Buttons:** 14 x ¾"/2 cm 4-hole buttons
- **Hook:** M/13 (9.00 mm)

gauge
Using M/13 (9.00 mm) hook approx 10 sts and 11 rows over 4"/10 cm of single crochet

abbreviations
See page 125

Right hand glove

Using M/13 (9.00 mm) hook make 23ch.

Row 1: 1ch, 1sc into 2nd ch from hook, 1sc into each ch to end, turn. (23 sts)

Row 2: 1ch, 1sc into 1st sc, 1sc into each sc to end, turn.

Row 3: 1ch, 1sc into 1st sc, 2ch, skip 2sc, 1sc into each sc to end, turn.

Row 4: 1ch, 1sc into next 20sc, 2sc into 2ch sp, 1sc into last sc, turn.

Row 5: As row 2.

Row 6: 1ch, 1sc into next 20sc, 2ch, skip 2sc, 1sc into last sc, turn.

Row 7: 1ch, 1sc into 1st sc, 2sc into 2ch sp, 1sc into each sc to end, turn.

Row 8: As row 2.

Repeat rows 3–8 twice more and rows 3–5 once more.

Row 24 (WS): 1ch, 1sc into next 20sc, turn.
Work on these 20 sts only.

Shape for thumb

Row 25: 1ch, 1sc into next 9sc, 2sc into next st, 1sc into next sc, 2sc into next sc, 1sc into next 8sc, turn. (22 sts)

Row 26: 1ch, 1sc into next 8sc, 2sc into next sc, 1sc into next 3sc, 2sc into next sc, 1sc into next 9sc, turn. (24 sts)

Row 27: 1ch, 1sc into next 9sc, 2sc into next st, 1sc into next 5sc, 2sc into next sc, 1sc into next 8sc, turn. (26 sts)

Row 28: (WS) 1ch, 1sc into next 17 sts, turn.

Next row: 1ch, 1sc into next 9sc, turn.
Work on these 9 sts only.
Repeat last row three more times.
Break off yarn and fasten off leaving long enough tail to sew up thumb.
With WS facing rejoin yarn and work 1sc into each of the 9sc to end, turn.
Sew up thumb.

Next row: (RS) 1ch, 1sc into next 9sc, 3sc into base of thumb, 1sc into rem 8sc, turn. (20 sts)

Next row: 1ch, 1sc into each sc to end, turn.
Repeat last row 8 more times.
Break off yarn and fasten off.

to finish

With right side facing, sew up side seam from top to base of thumb, leave 3sts and button flap open.
Sew buttons onto cuff matching up with button holes.
Sew in all loose ends.

Left hand glove

Using M/13 (9.00 mm) hook make 23ch.

Row 1: 1ch, 1sc into 2nd ch from hook, 1sc into each ch to end, turn. (23 sts)

Row 2: 1ch, 1sc into 1st sc, 1sc into each sc to end, turn.

Row 3: 1ch, 1sc into next 20sc, 2ch, skip 2sc, 1sc into last sc, turn.

Row 4: 1ch, 1sc into 1st sc, 2sc into 2ch sp, 1sc into each sc to end, turn.

Row 5: As row 2.

Row 6: 1ch, 1sc into 1st sc, 2ch, skip 2sc, 1sc into each sc to end, turn.

Row 7: 1ch, 1sc into next 20sc, 2sc into 2ch sp, 1sc into last sc, turn.

Row 8: As row 2.

Repeat rows 3–8 twice more and rows 3–5 once more.

Row 24: (WS) Sl st across first 3sc, 1ch, 1sc into each sc to end. (20 sts)

Shape for thumb

Row 25: 1ch, 1sc into next 8sc, 2sc into next st, 1sc into next sc, 2sc into next sc, 1sc into next 9sc, turn (22 sts).

Row 26: 1ch, 1sc into next 9sc, 2sc into next sc, 1sc into next 3sc, 2sc into next sc, 1sc into next 8sc, turn (24 sts).

Row 27: 1ch, 1sc into next 8sc, 2sc into next st, 1sc into next 5sc, 2sc into next sc, 1sc into next 9sc, turn. (26 sts)

Row 28: (WS) 1ch, 1sc into next 18sts, turn.

Next row: 1ch, 1sc into next 9sc, turn.

Work on these 9sts only.

Repeat last row 3 more times.

Break off yarn and fasten off, leaving long enough tail to sew up thumb.

With WS facing rejoin yarn and work 1sc into each of the 8sc to end, turn.

Sew up thumb.

Next row (RS): 1ch, 1sc into next 8sc, 3sc into base of thumb, 1sc into rem 9sc, turn. (20 sts)

Next row: 1ch, 1sc into each sc to end, turn.

Repeat last row 8 more times.

Break off yarn and fasten off.

to finish

With right side facing, sew up side seam from top to base of thumb, leave 3 sts and button flap open.

Sew buttons onto cuff matching up with button holes.

Sew in all loose ends.

beaded loop detail handbag

This bag has more than a touch of 1920s flapper inspiration. With beaded loops to the front and back, it will swing as you go. Worked in a neutral shade of organic DK weight cotton, the sparkly golden glass beads are really eye catching. The bag looks small but is deceptively deep – great for everyday use or a party.

star rating
★ ★ ★ (beginner)

finished size
Actual measurements: width 7¾"/20 cm; length 9½"/24 cm

materials
- **Yarn:** Rowan Organic DK Cotton Naturally Dyed, 100% organic cotton (approx 131 yd/20 m per 1.75 oz/50g ball)
- Oak apple, sh. 990 x 3 (brown)
- **Beads:** 4 x packets of beadworks 4.00 mm E beads – gold
- 1 x medium press stud
- **Hook:** G/6 (4.00 mm)

gauge
Using G/6 (4.00 mm) hook, approx 17 sts and 20 rows over 4"/10 cm of single crochet

abbreviations
bsc – beaded sc
See also page 125

Beaded loops (make 28)
Thread approximately 26 beads onto yarn.
Using G/6 (4.00 mm) hook make 24ch.
Row 1: 1ch, 1bsc into 2nd ch from hook, 1bsc into next 12ch, 1sc into each sc to end, turn. (24 sts)
Row 2: 1ch, 1sc into 1st sc, 1sc into each st to end, turn.
Row 3: 2ch, 1dc into each sc to end, turn.
Row 4: 1ch, 1sc into 1st dc, 1sc into each dc to end, turn.
Row 5: 1ch, 1bsc into 1st sc, 1bsc into next 13sc, 1sc into each sc to end.
Break off yarn and fasten off.

Bag panel (make 2)
Using G/6 (4.00 mm) hook make 35ch.
Row 1: 1ch, 1sc into 2nd ch from hook, 1sc into each ch from hook to end, turn. (35 sts)
Row 2: 1ch, 1sc into each sc to end, turn.
Rows 3-8: As row 2.
Row 9: 1ch, 1sc into 1st 3sc, attach beaded loop over next 5sc as follows: Fold loop in half with the beads to the front,** insert hook through both parts of loop, then into next sc, repeat from ** 4 more times, 1sc into next 3sc, * 5sc loop over next 5sc as previous loop, 1sc into next 3sc, rep from * to end, turn.
Rows 10-18: As row 2.
Row 19: 1ch, 1sc into 1st 7sc, *5sc loop over next 5sc, 1sc into next 3sc, rep from * to last 4sc, 1sc into last 4sc, turn.
Rows 20-28: As row 2.
Row 29: As row 9.
Rows 30-38: As row 2.
Row 39: 1ch, 1sc into 1st 2sc, sc2tog, 1sc into each sc to last 4sc, sc2tog, 1sc into last 2sc, turn. (33sts)
Row 40-42: As row 2.
Row 43: As row 39. (31sts)
Row 44: As row 2.
Row 45: 1ch, 1sc into 1st 5sc, *5sc loop over next 5sc, 1sc into next 3sc, rep from * to last 2sc, 1sc into last 2sc, turn.
Rows 46-56: As row 2.
Break off yarn and fasten off.

Bag handle
Using G/6 (4.00 mm) hook make 95ch.
Row 1: 1ch, 1sc into each ch to end, turn. (95 sts)
Row 2: 1ch, 1sc into 1st sc, 1sc into each sc to end, turn.
Rows 3-6: As row 2.
Break off yarn and fasten off.

to finish

Sew in all loose ends to WS of bag.
With RS together, sew base of front and back panels together using backstitch.
Sew front and back panels together at sides.
Fold last 5 rows of bag panel to the inside of bag, then pin and stitch approx 5 rows down to create an approx 1"/2.5 cm bagged trim at top.

Sew press stud to inside of bag approx 5 rows down from top. Use same yarn as for the bag: split a length if it's too thick to thread through the needle.
Pin handle to inside of bag evenly at side seams approx 1"/2.5 cm down from top and sew in place.

rose appliqué felted cushion

Pretty in pink, this felted cushion is really sweet. The cushion front is crocheted in one continuous piece with the neutral center stripe breaking up the two shades of pink. Appliqué rose buds echo the floral motifs on the backing fabric and pull the two sides beautifully together. Create matching cushions by playing about with the stripe sequence on the front panel.

star rating
★ ☆ ☆ (beginner)

finished size
Actual measurements: 17½"/44 cm square

materials
- **Yarn:** Rowan Scottish Tweed DK, 100% pure new wool (approx 109 yd/110 m per .8 oz/25 g ball)
  A – Brilliant pink, sh. 010 x 3
  B – Oatmeal, sh. 025 x 1
  C – Rose, sh. 026 x 2
  D – Gold, sh. 028 x 1
  Rowan Cotton Glace, 100% cotton (approx 125 yd/115 m per 1.75 oz/50 g ball) 3
  E – Ivy, sh. 812 x 1 (mid green)
  F – Shoot, sh. 814 x 1 (light green)
  G – Dijon, sh. 739 x 1 (brown/green)
- 20"/0.5 m of floral cotton fabric
- Sewing needle and cotton thread
- Cushion inner pad
- **Hooks:** D/3 (3.00 mm) and G/6 (4.00 mm)

gauge
After felting, using G/6 (4.00 mm) hook approx 16sts and 13 rows over 4"/10 cm of double crochets

abbreviations
See page 125

Front panel

Using G/6 (4.00 mm) hook and yarn A make 4ch, sl st into 1st chain to make a ring.

Round 1: 6ch (counts as 1dc and 3ch), *3dc into ring, 3ch, rep from * twice more, 2dc into ring, sl st into 3rd of 6ch at beg of round.

Round 2: Sl st into 6ch space, 6ch (counts as 1dc and 3ch), 1dc into same 6ch space, 1dc into top of next 3sts, 1dc into 3ch space, * 3ch, 1dc into same 3ch space, 1dc into top of next 3 sts, 1dc into next 3ch sp, rep from * once more, 3ch, 1dc into same 3ch space, 1dc into top of next 3 sts, sl st into 3rd ch of 6ch at beg of round.

Round 3: Sl st into 6ch space, 6ch (counts as 1dc and 3ch), 1dc into same 6ch space, 1dc into top of next 5 sts, 1dc into 3ch space, * 3ch, 1dc into same 3ch space, 1dc into top of next 5 sts, 1dc into next 3ch sp, rep from * once more, 3ch, 1dc into same 3ch space, 1dc into top of next 5 sts, sl st into 3rd ch of 6ch at beg of round.

Round 4: Sl st into 6ch space, 6ch (counts as 1dc and 3ch), 1dc into same 6ch space, 1dc into top of next 7 sts, 1dc into 3ch space, * 3ch, 1dc into same 3ch space, 1dc into top of next 7 sts, 1dc into next 3ch sp, rep from * once more, 3ch, 1dc into same 3ch space, 1dc into top of next 7 sts, sl st into 3rd ch of 6ch at beg of round.

Round 5: Sl st into 6ch space, 6ch (counts as 1dc and 3ch), 1dc into same 6ch space, 1dc into top of next 9 sts, 1dc into 3ch space, * 3ch, 1dc into same 3ch space, 1dc into top of next 9 sts, 1dc into next 3ch sp, rep from * once more, 3ch, 1dc into same 3ch space, 1dc into top of the next 9 sts, sl st into 3rd ch of 6ch at beg of round.

Round 6: Sl st into 6ch space, 6ch (counts as 1dc and 3ch), 1dc into same 6ch space, 1dc into top of next 11 sts, 1dc into 3ch space, * 3ch, 1dc into same 3ch space, 1dc into top of next 11 sts, 1dc into next 3ch sp, rep from * once more, 3ch, 1dc into same 3ch space, 1dc into top of the next 11sts, sl st into 3rd ch of the 6ch at beg of round.

Round 7: Sl st into 6ch space, 6ch (counts as 1dc and 3ch), 1dc into same 6ch space, 1dc into top of next 13 sts, 1dc into 3ch space, * 3ch, 1dc into same 3ch space, 1dc into top of next 13sts, 1dc into next 3ch sp, rep from * once more, 3ch, 1dc into same 3ch space, 1dc into top of next 13 sts, sl st into 3rd ch of the 6ch at beg of round.

Round 8: Sl st into 6ch space, 6ch (counts as 1dc and 3ch), 1dc into same 6ch space, 1dc into top of next 15sts, 1dc into 3ch space, * 3ch, 1dc into same 3ch space, 1dc into top of next 15 sts, 1dc into next 3ch sp, rep from * once more, 3ch, 1dc into same 3ch space, 1dc into top of next 15 sts, sl st into 3rd ch of 6ch at beg of round.

Round 9: Sl st into 6ch space, 6ch (counts as 1dc and 3ch), 1dc into same 6ch space, 1dc into top of next 17 sts, 1dc into 3ch space, * 3ch, 1dc into same 3ch space, 1dc into top of next 17 sts, 1dc into next 3ch sp, rep from * once more, 3ch, 1dc into same 3ch space, 1dc into top of next 17 sts, sl st into 3rd ch of 6ch at beg of round.

Round 10: Sl st into 6ch space, 6ch (counts as 1dc and 3ch), 1dc into same 6ch space, 1dc into top of next 19 sts, 1dc into 3ch space, * 3ch, 1dc into same 3ch space, 1dc into top of next 19 sts, 1dc into next 3ch sp, rep from * once more, 3ch, 1dc into same 3ch space, 1dc into top of the next 19 sts, sl st into 3rd ch of the 6ch at beg of round.
Work a further 10 rounds in yarn A and keep increasing as set in previous rows throughout.
Break off yarn A and join in yarn B.
Work a further 3 rounds in yarn B.
Break off yarn B and join in yarn C.
Work a further 7 rounds in yarn C.
Break off yarn and fasten off.
Sew in all loose ends.

Felting front panel

Using a cotton yarn, fold cushion panel in half with WS together and stitch together with a running stitch. This will help to keep its shape when being felted.
Using the spiky side of hook-and-loop tape, gently fluff up outer surface of cushion to raise the pile and help the fabric felt.
Place in the washing machine and wash at 40 degrees. Putting a pair of jeans or a similar heavy fabric in with it helps the felting process. Do not put in towels, however, as they will get covered in lint. You may need to repeat the felting process to achieve correct size.

Leaf (make 3 - 1 each in yarn E, F, and G).
Using D/3 (3.00 mm) hook and yarn E make 12ch.

Row 1: 1sc into 2nd ch from hook, 1sc into next 9ch, 3sc into last ch, then work back along other side of base chain with 1sc into next 8ch, turn.

Row 2: 1ch, 1sc into 1st sc, 1sc into next 8sc, 3sc into next sc, 1sc into next 9sc, turn.

Row 3: 1ch, 1sc into 1st sc, 1sc into next 9sc, 3sc into next sc, 1sc into next 8sc, turn.

Row 4: 1ch, 1sc into 1st sc, 1sc into next 8sc, 3sc into next sc, 1sc into next 9sc, turn.

Row 5: 1ch, 1sc into 1st sc, 1sc into next 9sc, 3sc into next sc, 1sc into next 8sc, turn.

Row 6: 1ch, 1sc into 1st sc, 1sc into next 8sc, 3sc into next sc, 1sc into next 9sc, turn.

Row 7: 1ch, 1sc into 1st sc, 1sc into next 10sc, sl st into next sc.
Break off yarn and fasten off.
Sew in loose ends.

Flower (make 3)
Using D/3 (3.00 mm) hook and yarn D make 45ch.

Row 1: 1ch, 1sc into 2nd ch from hook, 1sc into each ch to end, turn. (45 sts)

Row 2: 3ch (counts as 1st dc), skip 1st sc, 2dc into each sc to end, turn. (89 sts)

Row 3: 1ch, 1sc into1st dc, * skip 3dc, 7dc into next dc, skip 3dc, 1sc into next dc, rep from * to end working last sc into top of 3ch at beg of previous row.
Break off yarn and fasten off.
Sew in loose ends.
Roll flower up into a cone shape, and stitch base to secure.
Using the photograph as a guide, stitch leaves and flowers into place on front panel.

Back fabric panel
Cut fabric approx 1"/2.5 cm wider than front panel.
With WS facing fold in a 1"/2.5 cm seam around outer edge of cotton fabric and press with iron on the steam setting to form crease. Pin to outer edge of cushion and using hem stitch, sew 3 sides of cushion, insert cushion pad, then stitch last side.

square in the round blanket

When winter sets in, nothing beats snuggling up under a warm blanket with a hot drink and a good book. This blanket is ideal; each square is made up of the same basic pattern but given a slightly different look by simply changing the color at different places on the rounds. Although this is a large project, each square is worked separately so it is a great project to pick up whenever you have a spare moment.

star rating
★ ☆ ☆ (beginner)

finished size
Actual measurements: width 34"/87 cm; length 58"/148 cm

materials
- **Yarn:** Rowan Siena, 4ply mercerized cotton (approx 153 yd/140 m per 1.75 oz/50 g ball)
  A – Mariner, sh. 672 x 3 (bright blue)
  B – Celadan, sh. 669 x 3 (pale blue)
  C – Chill, sh. 666 x 3 (red)
  D – Oak, sh. 659 x 3 (mid green)
  E – Cream, sh. 652 x 3
  F – Pasture, sh. 654 x 3 (pale green)
- **Hook:** G/6 (4.00 mm)

gauge
1 x 10 row square measures 6¾"/17 cm

abbreviations
See page 125

Stripe sequence of squares (make 2 of each):

1	3 red, 2 celadan, 1 cream, 4 mariner
2	4 mariner, 1 red, 5 celadan
3	5 red, 2 cream, 1 celadan, 2 oak
4	6 celadan, 2 oak, 2 red
5	6 cream, 2 red, 2 mariner
6	6 red, 4 celadan
7	5 cream, 5 oak
8	5 green, 1 cream, 4 red
9	3 oak, 5 red, 2 blue
10	5 green, 1 red, 4 celadan
11	5 celadan, 3 mariner, 2 oak
12	3 mariner, 4 celadan, 3 red
13	5 oak, 5 mariner
14	7 red, 1 cream, 2 celadan
15	3 celadan, 3 red, 4 oak
16	5 mariner, 2 oak, 3 red
17	6 celadan, 4 mariner
18	5 cream, 5 celadan
19	5 mariner, 5 oak
20	6 celadan, 4 red

Basic square pattern (work 40 squares in total)

Using G/6 (4.00 mm) hook make 4ch, sl st into 1st ch to make a ring.

Round 1: 6ch (counts as 1dc and 3ch), *3dc into ring, 3ch, rep from * twice more, 2dc into ring, sl st into 3rd of the 6ch at beg of round.

Round 2: Sl st into next 3ch sp, 6ch (counts as 1dc and 3ch), 1dc into same 3ch sp, 1dc into next 3 sts, 1dc into next 3ch space, * 3ch, 1dc into same 3ch sp, 1dc into next 3 sts, 1dc into next 3ch sp, rep from * once more, 3ch, 1dc into same 3ch sp, 1dc into next 3 sts, sl st into 3rd of 6ch at beg of round.

Round 3: Sl st into 3ch sp, 6ch (counts as 1dc and 3ch), 1dc into same 3ch sp, 1dc into next 5 sts, 1dc into next 3ch sp, * 3ch, 1dc into same 3ch sp, 1dc into next 5 sts, 1dc into next 3ch sp, rep from * once more, 3ch, 1dc into same 3ch sp, 1dc into next 5 sts, sl st into 3rd of 6ch at beg of round.

Round 4: Sl st into next 3 ch sp, 6ch (counts as 1dc and 3ch), 1dc into same 3ch sp, 1dc into next 7 sts, 1dc into next 3ch sp, * 3ch, 1dc into same 3ch sp, 1dc into next 7 sts, 1dc into next 3ch sp, rep from * once more, 3ch, 1dc into same 3ch sp, 1dc into next 7 sts, sl st into 3rd of 6ch at beg of round.

Round 5: Sl st into next 3ch sp, 6ch (counts as 1dc and 3ch), 1dc into same 3ch sp, 1dc into next 9 sts, 1dc into next 3ch sp, * 3ch, 1dc into same 3ch sp, 1dc into next 9 sts, 1dc into next 3ch sp, rep from * once more, 3ch, 1dc into same 3ch sp, 1dc into top of the next 9 sts, sl st into 3rd of 6ch at beg of round.

Round 6: Sl st into next 3ch sp, 6ch (counts as 1dc and 3ch), 1dc into same 3ch space, 1dc into next 11 sts, 1dc into next 3ch sp, * 3ch, 1dc into same 3ch sp, 1dc into next 11sts, 1dc into next 3ch sp, rep from * once more, 3ch, 1dc into same 3ch sp, 1dc into next 11sts, sl st into 3rd of 6ch at beg of round.

Round 7: Sl st into next 3ch sp, 6ch (counts as 1dc and 3ch), 1dc into same 3ch sp, 1dc into 13 sts, 1dc into next 3ch sp, * 3ch, 1dc into same 3ch sp, 1dc into next 13 sts, 1dc into next 3ch sp, rep from * once more, 3ch, 1dc into same 3ch sp, 1dc into top of the next 13 sts, sl st into 3rd of 6ch at beg of round.

Round 8: Sl st into next 3ch sp, 6ch (counts as 1dc and 3ch), 1dc into same 3ch sp, 1dc into next 15 sts, 1dc into next 3ch sp, * 3ch, 1dc into same 3ch sp, 1dc into top of next 15 sts, 1dc into next 3ch sp, rep from * once more, 3ch, 1dc into same 3ch sp, 1dc into top of the next 15 sts, sl st into 3rd of 6ch at beg of round.

Round 9: Sl st into next 3ch sp, 6ch (counts as 1dc and 3ch), 1dc into same 6ch sp, 1dc into top of the next 17sts, 1dc into next 3ch sp, * 3ch, 1dc into same 3ch sp, 1dc into top of next 17 sts, 1dc into next 3ch sp, rep from * once more, 3ch, 1dc into same 3ch sp, 1dc into top of the next 17 sts, sl st into 3rd of 6ch at beg of round.

Round 10: Sl st into next 3ch sp, 6ch (counts as 1dc and 3ch), 1dc into same 3ch sp, 1dc into top of the next 19 sts, 1dc into next 3ch sp, 3ch, * 1dc into same 3ch sp, 1dc into top of next 19 sts, 1dc into next 3ch sp, rep from * once more, 3ch, 1dc into same 3ch sp, 1dc into top of the next 19 sts, sl st into 3rd of 6ch at beg of round.

Break off yarn and fasten off.

to finish

Sew in all loose ends.
Block and press each square.
Using grid below, sew each square together:

1	2	3	4	5
6	7	8	9	10
11	12	13	14	15
16	17	18	19	20
5	10	15	12	1
2	11	8	13	6
3	16	9	14	19
4	17	18	7	20

Border

Using G/6 (4.00 mm) hook and yarn F join yarn to top of 5th square in corner 3ch sp.

Round 1: 2ch *1dc into each of the dc along outer edge of square, 1dc into 1st ch of 3ch space, 1dc into seam, 1dc into 1st ch of next 3ch sp, rep from * along outer edge working 3dc into corner 3ch sp place marker at center st of 3dc **, then rep from * to ** down left hand side of blanket, then along bottom edge of blanket and up right hand side of blanket, working 3dc into first sp of round (place marker at center st of 3dc) sl st into top of 2ch at beg of round.

Round 2: 2ch, *1dc into each dc to marker, 3dc into marked st, place marker at center st of 3dc, rep from * three more times, 1dc into next st, sl st into top of 2ch at beg of round.

Repeat round 2, three more times.
Break off yarn and fasten off.
Block and press.

potholders

These easy-to-make potholders are the perfect kitchen accessory. They are made using the single crochet stitch throughout and the curved edges are worked by using increasing and decreasing techniques at the edges. The soft but sturdy DK weight cotton is layered up with contrast pads.

star rating

★ ★ ★ (beginner)

finished size

Actual measurements: width 7"/18 cm; length 34"/82 cm

materials

- **Yarn:** Rowan Handknit Cotton, DK weight, 100 % cotton (approx 93 yd/85 m per 1.75 oz/50 g ball) ③
  A – Rosso, sh. 215 x 3 (Red)
  B – Turkish plum, sh. 277 x 1 (Navy)
- **Hooks:** G/6 (4.00 mm) and D/3 (3.00 mm)

gauge

Using G/6 (4.00 mm) hook approx 15.5 sts to 18 rows over 4"/10 cm of single crochet

abbreviations

See page 125

Back

Using G/6 (4.00 mm) hook and yarn A make 21ch

Row 1: 1ch, 1sc into 2nd ch from hook, 1sc into each ch to end, turn. (21 sts)

Row 2: 1ch, 1sc into 1st 2 sts, 2sc into next st, 1 sc into each st to last 3 sts, 2sc into next st, 1sc into next 2 sts, turn. (23 sts)

Row 3: As row 2. (25 sts)

Row 4: As row 2. (27 sts)

Row 5: 1ch, 1sc into 1st st, 1sc into each st to end, turn.

Work a further 139 rows as row 5.

Row 145: 1ch, 1sc into 1st 2sc, sc2tog as follows – insert hook into next st, yo and draw through (2 loops on hook), insert hook into next st, yo and draw through (3 loops on hook), yo hook and draw through all 3 loops, 1sc into each st to last 4 sts, sc2tog, 1sc into last 2 sts, turn. (25 sts)

Row 146: As row 145. (23 sts)

Row 147: As row 145. (21 sts)

Row 148: 1ch, 1sc into 1st st, 1sc into each st to end.

Break off yarn and fasten off.

Pockets (make 2)

Using G/6 (4.00 mm) hook and yarn A make 21ch.

Row1: 1ch, 1sc into 2nd ch from hook, 1sc into each ch to end, turn. (21 sts)

Row 2: 1ch, 1sc into 1st 2 sts, 2sc into next st, 1sc into each st to last 3 sts, 2sc into next st, 1sc into last 2sts, turn. (23 sts)

Row 3: As row 2. (25 sts)

Row 4: As row 2. (27 sts)

Row 5: 1ch, 1sc into 1st st, 1sc into each st to end, turn.

Work a further 30 rows as row 5.

Break off yarn and fasten off.

Contrast pads (make 2)

Using G/6 (4.00 mm) hook and yarn B make 19ch.

Row 1: 1ch, 1sc into 2nd ch from hook, 1sc into each ch to end, turn. (19 sts)

Row 2: 1ch, 1sc into 1st 2 sts, 2sc into next st, 1sc into each st to last 4 sts, 2sc into next st, 1sc into last 2 sts, turn. (21sts)

Row 3: As row 2. (23 sts)

Row 4: As row 2. (25 sts)

Row 5: 1ch, 1sc into 1st st, 1sc into each st to end, turn.

Work a further 26 rows as row 5.

Break off yarn and fasten off.

to finish

Sew in all loose ends, block and press pieces.

Place contrast pads at each end with curved ends matching approx 2 rows in from bottom edge.

Pin to fabric, and then stitch into place using backstitch.

Place pockets at opposite side from contrast pads and match up curved edges.

Pin to fabric and stitch into place around outer edge using sewing up method described in techniques section.

Outer edge contrast trim

Using D/3 (3.00 mm) hook and with pocket top facing rejoin yarn B to 1st sc on the right hand side top of pocket. Work around the outer edge of the potholders as follows. Work 1ch, then 1sc into top of each sc along top of pocket, then work 54sc evenly along the side edge towards the next pocket, work sc around st and turning chains, next work 1sc into each stitch along 2nd pocket top. Next fold potholders in half and place marker at center point, work approx 27sc along outer edge until you reach marker, make 10ch, then work a further 27sc along edge towards first pocket top. Finish round by working slip stitch into top of 1ch worked at the beg of the round.

Next round: 1ch, 1sc into each sc around outer edge until you reach loop, work 12 sc around loop, then 1sc into each remaining sc to end, sl st into top of ch at beg of round.

Sew in loose ends, and then gently press trim to flatten and stretch slightly.

crochet half apron

This project was inspired by a classic butcher's apron. The dark blue background won't show spills and splashes, and, as it's worked throughout in alternative rows of single crochet and extended single crochet, the fabric is compact yet flexible.

star rating
★ ★ ★ (beginner)

finished size
Actual measurements: width 25"/63 cm; length 16½"/42 cm

materials
- **Yarn:** Rowan Cotton Glace, 100% cotton (approx 126 yd/115 m per 1.75 oz/50 g ball)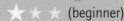
- A – Nightshade, sh. 246 x 6 (Blue)
- B – Poppy, sh. 741 x 1 (Red)
- C – Shoot, sh. 841 x 1 (Green)
- D – Bubbles, sh. 724 x 1 (Pink)
- **Hook:** D/3 (3.00 mm)

gauge
Using D/3 (3.00 mm) hook approx 20 sts and 18 rows over 4"/10 cm of pattern worked in 1 row sc and 1 row extended sc alternately

abbreviations
exsc – extended sc, worked as follows: Insert hook into stitch, yo and draw through, yo and draw under first loop on hook, yo and draw through both loops on hook
See also page 125

Stripe sequence worked throughout

1–6: A
7–8: B
9–14: A
15–16: C
17–22: A
23–24: D

Using D/3 (3.00 mm) hook and yarn A make 76ch.

Row 1: 1ch, 1sc into 2nd ch from hook, 1sc into each ch to end, turn. (76 sts)

Row 2: 1ch, 1exsc into 1st sc worked as follows: Insert hook into stitch, yo and draw through, yo and draw under first loop on hook, yo and draw through both loops on hook, work 1exsc into each st to end, turn.

Row 3: 1ch, 1sc into 1st exsc, 1sc into each exsc to last 2 sts, work 2sc into next st, 1sc into last st, turn. (77sts)

Row 4: 1ch, 1exsc into 1st st, 1exsc into each st to end, turn.

Row 5: 1ch, 1sc into 1st st, 1sc into each st to end, turn.

Row 6: 1ch, 1exsc into 1st st, 1exsc into each st to end, turn.

Break off yarn A and change to yarn B.

Row 7: 1ch, 1sc into 1st st, 1sc into each st to last 2 sts, work 2sc into next st, 1sc into last st, turn. (78sts)

Row 8: 1ch, 1exsc into 1st st, 1exsc into each st to end, turn.

Break off yarn B and change to yarn A.

Row 9: 1ch, 1sc into 1st st, 1sc into each st to end, turn.

Row 10: 1ch, 1exsc into 1st st, 1exsc into each st to end, turn.

Row 11: 1ch, 1sc into 1st st, 1sc into each st to last 2 sts, work 2sc into next st, 1sc into last st, turn. (79sts)

Row 12: 1ch, 1exsc into 1st st, 1exsc into each st to end, turn.

Row 13: 1ch, 1sc into 1st st, 1sc into each st to end, turn.

Row 14: 1ch, 1exsc into 1st st, 1exsc into each st to end, turn.

Break off yarn A and change to yarn C.

Row 15: 1ch, 1sc into 1st st, 1sc into each st to last 2 sts, work 2sc into next st, 1sc into last st, turn. (80sts)

Row 16: 1ch, 1exsc into 1st st, 1exsc into each st to end, turn.

Break off yarn C and change to yarn A.

Row 17: 1ch, 1sc into 1st st, 1sc into each st to end, turn.

Row 18: 1ch, 1exsc into 1st st, 1exsc into each st to end, turn.

Row 19: 1ch, 1sc into 1st st, 1sc into each st to last 2 sts, work 2sc into next st, 1sc into last st, turn. (81sts)

Row 20: 1ch, 1exsc into 1st st, 1exsc into each st to end, turn.

Row 21: 1ch, 1sc into 1st st, 1sc into each st to end, turn.

Row 22: 1ch, 1exsc into 1st st, 1exsc into each st to end, turn.

Break off yarn A and change to yarn D.

Row 23: 1ch, 1sc into 1st st, 1sc into each st to last 2 sts, work 2sc's into next st, 1sc into last st, turn. (82sts)

Row 24: 1ch, 1exsc into 1st st, 1exsc into each st to end, turn.

Break off yarn D and change to yarn A.

Row 25: 1ch, 1sc into 1st st, 1sc into each st to end, turn.

Row 26: 1ch, 1exsc into 1st st, 1exsc into each st to end, turn.

Row 27: 1ch, 1sc into 1st st, 1sc into each st to last 2 sts, work 2sc into next st, 1sc into last st, turn. (83sts)

Row 28: 1ch, 1exsc into 1st st, 1exsc into each st to end, turn.

Row 29: 1ch, 1sc into 1st st, 1sc into each st to end, turn.

Row 30: 1ch, 1exsc into 1st st, 1 exsc into each st to end, turn.

Break off yarn A and change to yarn B.

Row 31: 1ch, 1sc into 1st st, 1sc into each st to last 2 sts, work 2sc into next st, 1sc into last st, turn. (84sts)

Row 32: 1ch, 1exsc into 1st st, 1exsc into each st to end, turn.

Break off yarn B and change to yarn A.

Row 33: 1ch, 1sc into 1st st, 1sc into each st to end, turn.

Row 34: 1ch, 1exsc into 1st st, 1exsc into each st to end, turn.

Row 35: 1ch, 1sc into 1st st, 1sc into each st to last 2 sts, work 2sc into next st, 1sc into last st, turn. (85 sts)

Row 36: 1ch, 1exsc into 1st st, 1exsc into each st to end, turn.

Row 37: 1ch, 1sc into 1st st, 1sc into each st to end, turn.

Row 38: 1ch, 1exsc into 1st st, 1 exsc into each st to end, turn.

Break off yarn A and change to yarn C.

Row 39: 1ch, 1sc into 1st st, 1sc into each st to end, turn.

Row 40: 1ch, 1exsc into 1st st, 1 exsc into each st to end, turn.

Break off yarn C and change to yarn A.

Row 41–84: Work pattern as set, keeping stripe sequence correct, ending after 4 rows in yarn A.

Row 85: 1ch, 1sc into 1st st, 1sc into each st to last 3sts, sc2tog over next 2 sts as follows:
Insert hook into st, yo and draw through, insert hook into next st, yo and draw through, yo and draw through 3 loops on hook, 1sc into last st, turn. (84sts)

Row 86: 1ch, 1exsc into 1st st, 1 exsc into each st to end, turn.

Break off yarn A and change to yarn C.

Row 87: 1ch, 1sc into 1st st, 1sc into each st to end, turn.

Row 88: 1ch, 1exsc into 1st st, 1 exsc into each st to end, turn.

Break off yarn C and change to yarn A.

Row 89: 1ch, 1sc into 1st st, 1sc into each st to last 3sts, sc2tog, 1sc into last st, turn. (83sts)

Row 90: 1ch, 1exsc into 1st st, 1exsc into each st to end, turn.

Row 91: 1ch, 1sc into 1st st, 1 sc into each st to end, turn.

Row 92: 1ch, 1exsc into 1st st, 1exsc into each st to end, turn.

Row 93: 1ch, 1sc into 1st st, 1sc into each st to last 3sts, sc2tog, 1sc into last st, turn. (82sts)

Row 94: 1ch, 1exsc into 1st st, 1 exsc into each st to end, turn.

Break off yarn A and change to yarn D.

Row 95: 1ch, 1sc into 1st st, 1sc into each st to end, turn.

Row 96: 1ch, 1exsc into 1st st, 1 exsc into each st to end, turn.
Break off yarn D and change to yarn A.
Row 97: 1ch, 1sc into 1st st, 1sc into each st to last 3sts, sc2tog, 1sc into last st, turn. (81sts)
Row 98: 1ch, 1exsc into 1st st, 1exsc into each st to end, turn.
Row 99: 1ch, 1sc into 1st st, 1sc into each st to end, turn.
Row 100: 1ch, 1exsc into 1st st, 1exsc into each st to end, turn.
Row 101: 1ch, 1sc into 1st st, 1sc into each st to last 3sts, sc2tog, 1sc into last st, turn. (80sts)
Row 102: 1ch, 1exsc into 1st st, 1 exsc into each st to end, turn.
Break off yarn A and change to yarn B.
Row 103: 1ch, 1sc into 1st st, 1sc into each st to end, turn.
Row 104: 1ch, 1exsc into 1st st, 1 exsc into each st to end, turn.
Break off yarn B and change to yarn A.
Row 105: 1ch, 1sc into 1st st, 1sc into each st to last 3sts, sc2tog, 1sc into last st, turn. (79sts)
Row 106: 1ch, 1exsc into 1st st, 1exsc into each st to end, turn.
Row 107: 1ch, 1sc into 1st st, 1 sc into each st to end, turn.
Row 108: 1ch, 1exsc into 1st st, 1exsc into each st to end, turn.
Row 109: 1ch, 1sc into 1st st, 1sc into each st to last 3sts, sc2tog, 1sc into last st, turn. (78sts)
Row 110: 1ch, 1exsc into 1st st, 1 exsc into each st to end, turn.
Break off yarn A and change to yarn C.
Row 111: 1ch, 1sc into 1st st, 1sc into each st to end, turn.
Row 112: 1ch, 1exsc into 1st st, 1 exsc into each st to end, turn.
Break off yarn C and change to yarn A.
Row 113: 1ch, 1sc into 1st st, 1sc into each st to last 3sts, sc2tog, 1sc into last st, turn. (77sts)
Row 114: 1ch, 1exsc into 1st st, 1exsc into each st to end, turn.
Row 115: 1ch, 1sc into 1st st, 1 sc into each st to end, turn.
Row 116: 1ch, 1exsc into 1st st, 1exsc into each st to end, turn.
Row 117: 1ch, 1sc into 1st st, 1sc into each st to last 3sts, sc2tog, 1sc into last st, turn. (76sts)

Row 118: 1ch, 1exsc into 1st st, 1 exsc into each st to end.
Break off yarn and fasten off.

Pocket
Using yarn A and D/3 (3.00 mm) hook make 62ch.
Row 1: 1ch, 1sc into 2nd ch from hook, 1sc into each ch to end, turn. (62 sts)
Row 2: 1ch, 1exsc into 1st st, 1exsc into each sc to end, turn.
Repeat the 2 pattern rows throughout working in stripe sequence as shown at beg of pattern until row 24 has been worked, then repeat rows 1–14 again.
Break off yarn and fasten off.

Apron ties
Using yarn A and D/3 (3.00 mm) hook make 11ch.
Row 1: 1ch, 1sc into 2nd ch from hook, 1sc into each ch to end, turn. (11 sts)
Row 2: 1ch, 1sc into 1st st, 1sc into each st to end, turn.
Repeat row 2 until work measures 98½"/250 cm.
Break off yarn and fasten off.

to finish

Sew in loose ends to WS of work, block and press all pieces.
Pocket: Pin pocket to front of apron with last row at the top for the pocket opening and approx 18sts from top of main apron. Stitch into place using yarn A and backstitch.
Apron tie: Tie is approximately 2"/5 cm wide. Fold the tie in half so it measures approx 1"/2.5 cm, then press gently to form a crease. Next, mark the centerpoint, approx 49"/125 cm from the edge and match up with the center point of the top of the apron, approx 12½"/31.5 cm from the edge. Pin fabric into position, then stitch into place using backstitch.

outdoor cushion

This cushion is perfect for lazy summer afternoons in the garden or even to take on a picnic. The yarn used is a blend of silk and cotton, which is soft yet durable so ideal for outdoors.

star rating

★ ☆ ☆ (beginner)

finished size

Actual measurements: 18"/45 cm square

materials

- **Yarn:** Rowan Summer Tweed, aran weight, 70% silk and 30% blend
  A – Rush, sh. 507 x 3 (green)
  B – Reed, sh. 514 x 3 (oatmeal)
- Buttons x 4
- **Hook:** G/6 (4.00 mm)

gauge

Using G/6 (4.00 mm) hook approx 19 sts and 16 rows over 4"/10 cm of pattern

abbreviations

See page 125

Textured Squares

Make 4 in yarn A and 4 in yarn B.
Using G/6 (4.00 mm) make 39ch.
Row 1: 1ch, 1sc into 2nd ch from hook, 1sc into each ch to end, turn. (39sts)
Row 2: 1ch, 1sc into 1st sc, * 1ch, skip 1sc, 1sc into next sc, rep from * to end, turn.
Row 3: 2 ch, skip 1st sc, 1sc into 1st ch sp, * 1ch, skip next sc, 1sc into next ch sp, rep from * to 1st, 1sc into last sc, turn.
Row 4: 1ch, 1sc into 1st sc, * 1ch, skip 1sc, 1sc into next sc, rep from * to end.
Repeat last 2 rows 13 times, then row 3 once more.
Next row: 1ch, 1sc into 1st sc, * 1sc into ch sp, 1sc into next sc, rep from * to end.
Break off yarn and fasten off.

Cushion flap

Make 1 in yarn A and 1 in yarn B.
Work as given for textured square for rows 1–3.
Place button holes.
Row 4: 1ch, skip 1st sc, 1sc into ch sp, (1ch, skip 1sc, 1sc into next ch sp) 3 times, 3ch, skip (1sc, 1ch sp and 1sc) (1sc into next ch sp, 1ch, skip 1sc) 9 times, 2ch, skip (1ch sp and 1sc) * 1sc into next ch sp, 1ch, skip 1sc, rep from * to end working last sc into tch at end of row, turn.
Repeat row 3 from textured square a further 10 times.
Next row: 1ch, 1sc into 1st sc, * 1sc into ch sp, 1sc into next sc, rep from * to end.
Break off yarn and fasten off.

to finish

Sew in all loose ends.
Block and press squares.

Make up front and back cushion panels as follows:
Using the photo as a guide, make check pattern with 4 squares, stitch together.
Sew base and side seams together, leaving top open. Sew 2 flap rectangles together and then stitch to front panel. Sew buttons onto back panel to match up with button holes.

crochet hook case

This project is a great way to practice the basic single crochet stitch, as well as changing color and keeping edges straight. The stripes in the design mean it uses very little yarn so is perfect for using up scraps left over from other projects. The only thing to remember is to make sure the yarns are all the same weight. If you like, you could also add a bit of embroidery to the front or even a couple of contrasting buttons — let your imagination run wild!

star rating
★ ☆ ☆ (beginner)

finished size
Actual measurements: width 4"/10.5 cm; length 12½"/31.5 cm

materials
- **Yarn:** Rowan Kid Silk Haze, DK weight, 100% cotton (approx 93 yd/85 m per 1.75 oz/50 g ball)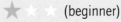
  A – Delphinium, sh. 334 x 1 (Lilac)
  B – Slick, sh. 313 x 1 (Pink)
  C – Tangerine, sh. 337 x 1 (Orange)
  D – Sunflower, sh. 336 x 1 (Yellow)
  E – Pesto, sh. 344 x 1 (Green)
- **Hook:** G/6 (4.00 mm)
- **Fabric:** 1 x rectangle of felt fabric approx 9½ x 12"/(24 x 30 cm)
- 8"/20 cm elastic cord
- 2 x large buttons
- Needle and sewing cotton

gauge
Using a G/6 (4.00 mm) hook approx 16 sts and 18 rows over 4"/10 cm of single crochet

abbreviations
See page 125

Using D/3 (3.00 mm) hook and yarn A make 54ch.
Be careful not to make the chain too tight.
Row 1: 1ch, 1sc into 2nd ch from hook, 1sc into each ch to end, turn. (54 sts)
Row 2: 1ch, 1sc into 1st st, 1sc into each st to end, turn.
Rows 3-4: As row 2.
Break off yarn A and change to yarn B.
Rows 5-8: As row 2.
Break off yarn B and change to yarn C.
Rows 9-12: As row 2.
Break off yarn C and change to yarn D.
Rows 13-16: As row 2.
Break off yarn D and change to yarn E.
Rows 17-20: As row 2.
Break off yarn, fasten off and sew in the loose ends.

Block and press crochet fabric

Cut 2 rectangles from felt fabric – one measuring 4 x 12¼"/10 x 31cm and one 4 x 5½"/10 x 14 cm.
Pin the smaller rectangle to the bottom of the larger one and sew into position around the outer edge to secure. Be sure to leave the top section open, as this will be the pocket for your crochet hooks. Divide the pocket into 3 even sections by stitching from the top of the opening to the bottom, using either backstitch or a running stitch. Use pins as a guide to ensure you sew in a straight line.

Cut the elastic cord in half and knot the ends together to form 2 loops. Pin them to WS or to what will be the inside of the hook case at center bottom of the 2nd and 4th stripe.

Place the felt fabric (pocket side up) onto the crochet fabric and pin into position. Stitch around the outside edge with either back or running stitch. When you come to the elastic loops, remember to remove the pins and stitch over the elastic a few times extra to make it really secure.

Fold the hook case in half lengthwise and sew buttons onto the outside to match up with the elastic cord loops.

Tip To save having to sew in loose ends, try working them in as you go along. When inserting your hook into the stitch, holding the loose ends close to the top of the work (over the top of the hook), work the stitch as you would normally, and the loose ends should become trapped in the fabric.

knitting needle case

This case keeps all your knitting needles together in a safe place. It's a square with a slight twist, worked by increasing and decreasing on the outer edges. The stripes automatically create a diagonal stripe which, when rolled up, adds an interesting touch.

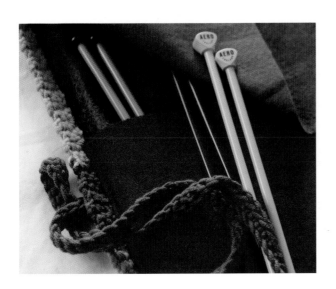

star rating

★ ★ ★ (beginner)

finished size

Actual measurement: 16"/40 cm square

materials

- **Yarn:** Rowan All Seasons Cotton, aran weight, 60% cotton 40% acrylic (approx 97 yd/89 m per 1.75 oz/50 g ball)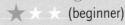
  A – Cement, sh. 235 x 1 (Grey)
  B – Wisteria, sh. 229 x 1 (Lilac)
  C – Scarlet, sh. 236 x 1 (Red)
- Nylon felt fabric
  Purple – 14 x 15"/36 x 38 cm
  Red – 14 x 9 ½"/36 x 24 cm
  Grey – 14 x 7"/36 x 18 cm
- **Hook:** G/6 (4.00 mm)

gauge

Using G/6 (4.00 mm) hook approx 15 sts and 18 rows over 4"/10 cm of single crochet

abbreviations

Sc2tog – work 2 single crochet 2 together
Sc3tog – work 2 single crochet 3 together
See also page 125

Stripe sequence

Rows 1–16: Grey
Rows 17–21: Lilac
Rows 22–29: Red
Rows 30–33: Grey
Rows 34–39: Lilac
Rows 40–58: Red
Rows 59–60: Grey
Rows 61–64: Lilac
Rows 65–66: Red
Rows 67–68: Grey
Rows 69–72: Lilac
Rows 73–74: Red
Rows 75–76: Grey
Rows 77–80: Lilac
Rows 81–82: Red
Rows 83–84: Grey
Rows 85–88: Lilac
Rows 89–90: Red
Rows 91–92: Grey
Rows 93–96: Lilac
Rows 97–98: Red
Rows 99–103: Grey

Using G/6 (4.00 mm) hook and yarn A make 3ch.
Row 1: Work 3sc into 1st ch made, turn. (3 sts)
Row 2: 1ch, 1sc into 1st sc, 3sc into next sc, 1sc into last sc, turn. (5 sts)
Row 3: 1ch, 1sc into 1st sc, 2sc into next sc, 1sc into next sc, 2sc into next sc, 1sc into last sc, turn. (7 sts)
Row 4: 1ch, 1sc into 1st sc, 2sc into next sc, 1sc into next 3sc, 2sc into next sc, 1sc into last sc, turn. (9 sts)
Row 5: 1ch, 1sc into 1st sc, 2sc into next sc, 1sc into each st to last 2 sts, 2sc into next sc, 1sc into last sc, turn. (11 sts)
Row 6: 1ch, 1sc into each st to end, turn.
Following stripe sequence, keep increasing as set for 4 rows, and then work one row even until there are 81 sts.
Row 50: 1ch, 1sc into 1st sc, sc2tog, 1sc into each st to last 3 sts, sc2tog, 1sc into last sc, turn. (79 sts)
Row 51: 1ch, 1sc into 1st sc, sc2tog, 1sc into each st to last 3sts, sc2tog, 1sc into last sc, turn. (77 sts)

Row 52: 1ch, 1sc into 1st sc, sc2tog, 1sc into each st to last 3 sts, sc2tog, 1sc into last sc, turn. (75 sts)
Row 53: 1ch, 1sc into 1st sc, sc2tog, 1sc into each st to last 3 sts, sc2tog, 1sc into last sc, turn. (73 sts)
Row 54: 1ch, 1sc into each st to end, turn.
Keep decreasing as set for 4 rows, and then work one row even until 5 sts remain.
Next row: 1ch, 1sc, sc3tog, 1sc, turn. (3 sts)
Next row: 1ch, sc3tog. (1 st)
Break off yarn and fasten off.

Strap
Using yarn C and G/6 (4.00 mm) hook make 100ch.
Row 1: 1ch, 1sc into each ch to end.
Break off yarn and fasten off.

to finish

Sew in loose ends.
Block and press diagonal stripe crochet square.
Cut felt fabric to sizes below:
1 x Red: 13¾ x 9"/35 cm x 23 cm
1x Purple: 13¾ x 14"/35 cm x 36 cm
1 x Grey: 13¾ x 6¾"/35 cm x 17 cm

Pin red rectangle to the bottom of the purple one and sew into position around the outer edge to secure, leave the top section open as this will be the pocket for your knitting needles. Then divide the pocket up into 5 even sections by stitching from the top of the opening to the bottom either using backstitch or a running stitch. Use pins to create a straight line as a guide.
Pin grey rectangle to the top of purple one and sew into position for flap.
Place purple section onto crochet fabric with pockets and flap facing you and stitch to crochet fabric using backstitch.
Turn case over so the crochet fabric is facing, fold strap in half and stitch to half way point on front of case.

big button shopper

This cute bag is quick and simple to make, worked in a single crochet stitch throughout to give a dense compact fabric when felted. It's big enough to carry all your essentials and durable enough to handle any type of adventure – shopping or otherwise!

star rating
★ ★ ★ (beginner)

finished size
Actual measurements: width 12½"/32 cm; length 15"/38 cm

materials
- **Yarn:** Rowan Big Wool, 100% merino wool (approx 87 yd/80 m per 3.5 oz/100 g ball)
  A – Black, sh. 008 x 4
- Rowan Siena, 4ply mercerized cotton (approx 153 yd/140 m per 1.75 oz/50 g ball)
  B – Chilli, sh. 666 x 1 (red)
  C – Pacific, sh. 660 x 1 (turquoise)
  D – Oak, sh. 649 x 1 (green)
  E – Lustre, sh. 665 x 1 (yellow)
  F – Flounce, sh. 664 x 1 (pink)
- Small strip of hook-and-loop tape
- **Buttons:** 1 x large – 1"/3 cm, 3 x medium – ¾"/2 cm, 1 x small – ½"/1 cm
- **Hooks:** O/16 (12.00 mm) and 5/6 (1.75 mm)

gauge
Using O/16 (12.00 mm) hook approx 8 sts and 10.5 rows over 4"/10 cm of single crochet before felting

abbreviations
See page 125

Front and back panels
Using O/16 (12.00 mm) hook and yarn A make 28ch.
Row 1: 1ch, 1sc into 2nd ch from hook, 1sc into each ch to end, turn. (28 sts)
Row 2: 1ch, 1sc into each sc to end, turn.
Repeat row 2, 30 more times.
Break off yarn and fasten off.

Handle (make 2)
Using yarn A and O/16 (12mm) hook make 4ch.
Row 1: 1ch, 1sc into 2nd ch from hook, 1sc into each ch to end, turn. (4 sts)
Row 2: 1ch, 1sc into each sc to end, turn.
Repeat row 2 a further 47 times.
Break off yarn and fasten off.

to finish

Sew in all loose ends.
Pin and stitch front and back panels together leaving top open.
Sew handles to top opening of bag approximately 1 row down from the top and 3 sts in from the side seam.
Using a cotton yarn stitch bag opening together with a running stitch. This will help the bag keep it's shape when being felted.
Using the spiky side of hook-and-loop tape, gently fluff up outer surface of bag. This will raise the pile and help the bag felt.
Put in the washing machine and wash at 40 degrees. Putting a pair of jeans or similar heavy fabric will help the felting process. Do not put in with towels as they will get covered in lint!

Crochet discs
Make 4 large, 4 medium, 5 small in each color of 4ply cotton.
Make 3 medium in multi colors – 2 rounds yellow /1 round pink, 2 rounds turquoise/ 1 round red, 2 rounds red /1 round yellow.
Large disc
Using 5/6 (1.75 mm) hook make 4ch, sl st into 1st ch to make a ring.
Round 1: 1ch, 8sc into ring, sl st into 1ch at beginning of round. (8 sts)
Round 2: 1ch, 2sc into each sc to end, sl st into 1ch at beg of round. (16 sts)
Round 3: 1ch, 1sc into 1st sc, 2sc into next sc,* 1sc into next sc, 2sc into next sc, rep from * to end, sl st into 1ch at beg of round. (24 sts)
Round 4: 1ch, 1 sc into 1st 2sc, 2sc into next sc,* 1sc into next 2sc, 2sc into next sc, rep from * to end, sl st into 1ch at beg of round. (32 sts)
Break off yarn and fasten off.
Medium disc: Work as above ending after round 3.
Small disc: Work as above ending after round 2.

Sew in loose ends.
Using the photographs as a guide, pin and sew discs onto front panel of bag, then sew buttons onto bag.

fuzzy felted spike scarf

This scarf is a real statement piece. The extra-long length allows you to tie it in lots of different ways, with the crochet spikes tumbling down like autumnal leaves falling from the trees. Worked in a soft wool, acrylic, and viscose blend using a large hook, it's light and beautifully soft next to the skin. The space dye effect in the yarn also means that each spike has a subtly different color to it.

star rating
★★☆ (intermediate)

finished size
Actual measurements: width 9¾"/25 cm; length 58¼"/148 cm

materials
- **Yarn:** Patons Shadow Tweed, chunky weight yarn, 58% wool 40% acrylic 4% viscose (approx 145 yd/133m per 3.5 oz/100g ball) 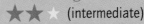 Red/brown mix, sh. 6906 x 2
- **Hook:** M/13 (9.00 mm)

gauge
Using M/13 (9.00 mm) hook approx 9 sts and 2 rows over 4"/10 cm (4 of linked double trebles

abbreviations
Ldc – linked double crochet
Ltr – linked treble
Ldtr – linked double treble
Ltrtr – linked triple treble
See also page 125

Scarf center is worked in one continuous row of linked triple trebles. The linked stitches are started off by working into the initial turning chain. This scarf is worked throughout with the RS facing. Using M/13 (9.00 mm) hook make 154ch. Insert hook into 2nd ch from hook, yo and pull through, (insert hook into next ch, yo and pull through) 3 times (5 loops on hook), (yo and draw through 1st 2 loops on hook) 4 times until 1 loop left on hook, first linked stitch is completed.

Work next and every stitch as follows:
*Insert hook down through 1st horizontal loop that is around 1st stitch, yo and draw through, insert hook down into 2nd horizontal loop, yo and draw through, insert hook into 3rd horizontal loop, yo and draw through, insert hook into next ch, yo and draw through, (5 loops on hook), (yo and draw through 1st 2 loops on hook) 4 times until 1 loop left on hook, rep from * to end of chain. Break off yarn and fasten off.

Make first spike as follows:

Using M/13 (9.00 mm) hook make 11ch.
1sc into 2nd ch from hook, 1hdc into next ch, 1Lhdc into next st as follows:
Insert hook down into horizontal loop at top of last stitch, yo and draw through, insert hook into next ch, yo and draw through – 3 loops on hook, yo and draw through 1st 2 loops – 2 loops on hook, yo and draw through 2 loops – 1 loop on hook, 1ch.,1Ltr as follows:
Insert hook down through front loop at top of last st, yo and draw through – 2 loops on hook – insert hook down into horizontal loop, yo and draw through – 3 loops on hook, insert hook into ch, yo and draw through – 4 loops on hook (yo and draw through 2 loops) 3 times – 1 loop on hook, 1ch, 1 Ldtr as follows:
Insert hook down through front loop at top of last stitch, yo and draw through – 2 loops on hook, insert hook down into next horizontal loop, yo and draw through) twice – 4 loops on hook, insert hook into next ch, yo and draw through – 5 loops on hook (yo and draw through 2 loops) 4 times – 1 loop on hook Ldtr into next 2ch, starting st by inserting hook into 1st horizontal loop of last st, 1ch, 1 Ltrtr as follows:
Insert hook down through front loop at top of last

stitch, yo and draw through – 2 loops on hook (insert hook down into next horizontal loop, yo and draw through) 3 times – 5 loops on hook, insert into next ch, yo and draw through – 6 loops on hook (yo and draw through 2 loops) 5 times – 1 loop on hook, 1Ltrtr into next 2 ch, starting st by inserting hook into 1st horizontal loop of last st.

Then work 1sc into 1st ch of scarf center.

* Work 1 spike as above, skip 5 sts, 1sc into next ch, rep from * along outer edge of scarf until you reach end of 150ch, 1 spike, skip linked stitch, 1sc into top of 1st st ** 1 spike, skip 5 sts, 1sc into next st, rep from ** to end.
Break off yarn and fasten off.

to finish

Sew in all loose ends. Joins open base of spikes to center of scarf by linking horizontal loops of last linked stitch to the top of chains on 1st side and stitches on 2nd side.

Block and press.

cobweb lace gloves

These gloves are a real treat to wear. They use a kid mohair and silk blend yarn, which makes them incredibly soft and cozy.

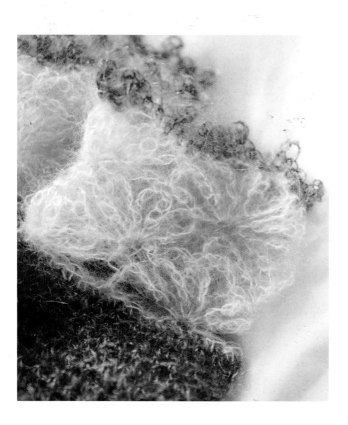

star rating
★★☆ (intermediate)

finished size
Actual measurements: width at thumb 4½"/11 cm; length 10"/25 cm

materials
- **Yarn:** Rowan Kid Silk Haze, 70% kid mohair 30% silk (approx 230 yd/210 m per .88 oz/25 g ball)
  A – Dewberry, sh. 600 x 2 (lilac)
  B – Mist, sh. 636 x 1 (pale blue)
- **Hooks:** H/8 (5.00 mm) and G/6 (4.00 mm)

gauge
Using G/6 (4.00 mm) hook approx 17 sts and 20 rows over 4"/10 cm of single crochet

abbreviations
TP – triple picot: work 1sc, [7ch, 1sc] 3 times all into the same place.
See also page 125

Left glove

Using H/8 (5.00 mm) hook and yarn A, make 42ch.

Change to G/6 (4.00 mm) hook.

Row 1: 1ch, 1sc into 2nd ch from hook and every foll ch to end, turn. (42 sts)

Row 2: 1ch, 1sc into 1st sc, 1sc into each sc to end, turn.

Row 3-4: As row 2.

Row 5: 1ch, 1sc into 1st sc, sc2tog over next 2 sts, 1sc into each sc to last 3 sts, sc2tog, 1sc, turn. (40 sts)

Row 6: As row 2.

Row 7: As row 5. (38 sts)

Rows 8-10: As row 2.

Repeat rows 7-10 twice more. (34 sts)

Row 19: As row 5. (32 sts)

Row 20-24: As row 2.

Row 25: As row 5. (30 sts)

Row 26-30: As row 2.

**Start shaping for thumb

Row 31: 1ch, 1sc into next 15 sts, 2sc into next st, 1sc into next st, 2sc into next st, 1sc into each st to the end, turn. (32 sts)

Row 32: 1ch, 1sc into 1st st, 1sc into each st to end, turn.

Row 33: 1ch, 1sc into next 15 sts, 2sc into next st, 1sc into next 3 sts, 2sc into next st, 1sc into each st to end, turn. (34 sts)

Row 34: As row 32.

Row 35: 1ch, 1sc into next 15 sts, 2sc into next st, 1sc into next 5 sts, 2sc into next st, 1sc into each st to end, turn. (36 sts)

Row 36: As row 32.

Row 37: 1ch, 1sc into next 15 sts, 2sc into next st, 1sc into next 7 sts, 2sc into next st, 1sc into each st to end, turn. (38 sts)

Row 38: As row 32.

Row 39: 1ch, 1sc into next 15 sts, 2sc into next st, 1sc into next 9 sts, 2sc into next st, 1sc into each st to end, turn. (40 sts)

Row 40: As row 32.

Row 41: 1ch, 1sc into next 28 sts, turn.

Row 42: 1ch, 1sc into 1st st, 1sc into next 12 sts, turn. (13 sts)

Work 8 rows of single crochet on these 13 sts only or until required length.

Break off yarn and fasten off.

Sew thumb side seam together. With RS facing rejoin yarn to left hand side of thumb and work 1sc into each st to end, turn.

Next row: 1ch, 1sc into next 15 sts, work 2sc evenly across base of thumb, 1sc into each st to end. (29 sts)

Daisy chain lace top

Break off yarn A and join in yarn B.

Row 1: 1ch, 1sc into each st to end, turn.

Row 2: 8ch, TP into the 4th sc (12th st from hook),* 4ch, skip 4sc, 1dc into next sc, ** 4ch, skip 4sc, TP into next sc, rep from * ending last rep at ** in last sc, turn.

Row 3: 1ch, 1sc into 1st st, *1ch, 1sc into first 7ch arch of next TP, [3ch, 1sc into next 7ch arch of same TP] twice, 1ch, skip 4ch, 1sc into next dc, repeat from * to end working last sc into arch of turning ch, turn.

Row 4: 8ch, work [1sc, 7ch, 1sc] into 1st sc, * 4ch, skip [1ch, 1sc and 3ch], 1dc into next sc, 4ch, skip [3ch, 1sc and 1ch]**, TP into next sc, rep from * ending last rep at **, work [1sc, 7ch, 1sc, 3ch and 1tr] into last sc, skip turning ch, turn.

Row 5: 1ch, 1sc into 1st st, 3ch, 1sc into next 7ch arch, *1ch, skip 4ch, 1sc into next dc, 1ch, 1sc into 1st 7ch arch of next TP **, [3ch, 1sc into next arch of same TP] twice; rep from * ending last rep at **, 3ch, 1sc into turning ch arch, turn.

Row 6: 7ch, skip [3ch, 1sc and 1ch], *TP into next sc, 4ch, skip [1ch, 1sc and 3ch], 1dc into next sc**, 4ch, skip [3ch, 1sc and 1ch];rep from * ending last rep at **, turn.

Row 7: As row 3. Break off yarn and fasten off.

Picot edge

The gloves are finished with a contrast picot edge along the top and bottom of the glove. The picot edge is worked in exactly the same way on both edges. Use yarn A for the top edge and yarn B for the bottom edge.

Top edge

With RS facing, insert hook into sc at beginning of row, make a slip knot in contrast yarn and place on hook, draw through, yo and draw through loop.

Row 1: 1ch, *1sc into next 3 sts, make picot as follows: 3ch, 1sl st into last sc worked, repeat from * to last st, 1sc into last st. Break off yarn and fasten off.

Row 32: 1ch, 1sc into 1st st, 1sc into each st to end, turn.

Row 33: 1ch, 1sc into next 12 sts, 2sc into next st, 1sc into next 3 sts, 2sc into next st, 1sc into each sc to end, turn. (34 sts)

Row 34: As row 32.

Row 35: 1ch, 1sc into next 12 sts, 2sc into next st, 1sc into next 5 sts, 2sc into next st, 1sc into each sc to end, turn. (36 sts)

Row 36: As row 32.

Row 37: 1ch, 1sc into next 12 sts, 2sc into next st, 1sc into next 7 sts, 2sc into next st, 1sc into each sc to end, turn. (38 sts)

Row 38: As row 32.

Row 39: 1ch, 1sc into next 12 sts, 2sc into next st, 1sc into next 9 sts, 2sc into foll st, 1sc into each sc to end, turn. (40 sts)

Row 40: As row 32.

Row 41: 1ch, 1sc into next 25 sts, turn.

Row 42: 1ch, 1sc into 1st st, 1sc into next 12 sts, turn. (13 sts)

Work 8 rows of single crochet on these 13 sts only or until required length.

Break off yarn and fasten off.

Sew thumb side seam together, with RS facing rejoin yarn to left hand side of thumb and work 1sc into each st to end, turn.

Next row: 1ch, 1sc into next 12 sts, work 2sc evenly across base of thumb, 1sc into each st to end. (29 sts)

Daisy Chain Lace top
Work as given for left glove.

Top and Bottom Picot edge
Work as given for left glove.

to finish

Sew in all loose ends then gently block and press.

Sew up side seams using flat seam technique as described on page 26.

Bottom edge
With RS facing, insert hook into 1st ch at beginning of 1st row, make a slip knot in contrast yarn and place on hook, draw through, yo and draw through loop.

Row 1: 1ch, *1sc into next 3ch, 1picot, repeat from * to end.
Break off yarn and fasten off.

Right glove
Work as given for left glove until ** shape for thumb.
Start shaping for thumb
Row 31: 1ch, 1sc into next 12 sts, 2sc into next st, 1sc into next st, 2sc into next st, 1sc into each st to end, turn. (32 sts)

drawstring halter top

This fresh halter top is perfect for day or night. It's crocheted throughout in a linen mix yarn, which gives the fabric a fantastic drape, while the textured stripes add a splash of color. The clever use of stitch and pattern make this design fun to crochet, and the button detail to the back gives the perfect finishing touch.

star rating
★★☆ (intermediate)

finished size
See chart page 126

materials
- **Yarn:** Rowan Lenpur Linen, Dk weight 75% VI Lenpur 25% Linen (approx 126 yd/115 m per 1.75 oz/50 g ball) [3]
  A – Tattoo, sh. 566 x 4, 5,5 6, 6 (grey)
  B – Lagoon, sh. 565 x 1 (turquoise)
  C – Jungle, sh. 569 x 1 (green)
  D – Saffron, sh. 561 x1 (orange)
  E – Vivid, sh. 563 x 1 (pink)
- 8 (9, 10, 11, 11) x 1 cm (⅓ in) shell buttons
- **Hooks:** G/6 (4.00 mm) and D/3 (3.00 mm)

gauge
Using G/6 (4.00 mm) hook 2 repeats of diamond lace pattern measures approx 4½"/11.5 cm

abbreviations
See page 125

Diamond lace panel

Using G/6 (4.00 mm) hook and yarn A work
41ch.

Row 1: 1ch, 1sc into 2nd ch from hook, 1sc into
each ch to end, turn. (41 sts)

Row 2: 1ch, 1sc into 1st sc, 1sc into each sc to
end, turn.

Row 3 (RS): 1ch, 1sc into 1st sc, 1sc into next
2sc, * 5ch, skip 3sc **, 1sc into next 5sc, rep
from * ending last rep at **, 1sc into last 3sc,
turn.

Row 4: 1ch, 1sc into 1st 2sc, , * 3ch, skip 1sc, 1sc
into next 5ch arch, 3ch, skip 1sc **, 1sc into each
of next 3sc, rep from * ending last rep at **, 1sc
into last 2sc, turn.

Row 5: 1ch, 1sc into 1st sc, * 3ch, skip 1sc, 1sc
into next 3ch sp, 1sc into next sc, 1sc into next
3ch sp, 3ch, skip 1sc, 1sc into next sc, rep from *
to end, turn.

Row 6: 5ch (counts as 1dc and 2ch), * 1sc into
next 3ch sp, 1sc into each of next 3sc, 1sc into
next 3ch sp, **, 5ch, rep from * ending last rep
at **, 2ch, 1dc into last sc, turn.

Row 7: 1ch, 1sc into 1st st, * 3ch, skip 1sc, 1sc
into each of next 3sc, 3ch, skip 1sc, 1sc into next
5ch arch, rep from * working last sc in tch, turn.

Row 8: 1ch, 1sc into 1st sc, * 1sc into next 3ch sp,
3ch, skip 1sc, 1sc into next sc, 3ch, skip 1sc, 1sc
into next 3ch sp, 1sc into next sc, rep from * to
end, turn.

Row 9: 1ch, 1sc into 1st 2sc, * 1sc into next 3ch
sp, 5ch, 1sc into next 3ch sp **, 1sc into each of
next 3sc, rep from * ending last rep at **, 1sc
into last 2sc, turn.

Row 10: 1ch, 1sc into 1st 3sc, *3sc into 5ch sp,
1sc into each of next 5sc, rep from * ending last
rep 1sc into each of last 3sc, turn.

Row 11: 1ch, 1sc into 1st st, 1sc into each sc to
end, turn.

Row 12: As row 11.

Repeat rows 4–12, 11 (12, 13, 14, 15) more times.
Break off yarn and fasten off.

Bodice

Work bodice along outer row-end edge of
diamond lace panel.

With RS facing and using G/4 (4.00 mm) hook,
rejoin yarn A to last sc of diamond lace panel.

Row 1: 1ch, work 132 (142, 154, 164, 176) sc
along outer row-end edge of diamond lace panel
(approx 11sc to each pattern repeat).

Row 2: 1ch, 1sc into each sc to end, turn.

Row 3: As row 2.

Do not break off yarn A, join in yarn B.

Row 4: 1ch, 1sc into each sc to end, turn.

Row 5: 1ch, 1sc into front loop of each sc to
end, turn.

Break off yarn B, rejoin yarn A.

Row 6–8: 1ch, 1sc into each sc to end, turn.

Do not break off yarn A, join in yarn C.

Row 9: 1ch, 1sc into each sc to end, turn.

Row 10: 1ch, 1sc into back loop of each sc to
end, turn.

Break off yarn B, rejoin yarn A.

Row 11–13: 1ch, 1sc into each sc to end, turn.

Do not break off yarn A, join in yarn D.

Row 14: 1ch, 1sc into each sc to end, turn.

Row 15: 1ch, 1sc into back loop of each sc to
end, turn.

Break off yarn D, rejoin yarn A.

Row 16–18: 1ch, 1sc into each sc to end, turn.

Do not break off yarn A, join in yarn E.

Row 19: 1ch,1sc into each sc to end, turn.

Row 20: 1ch, 1sc into front loop of each sc to
end, turn.

Break off yarn E, rejoin yarn A.

Row 21: 1ch, 1sc into each sc to end, turn.

Repeat last row 5 (5, 7, 7, 9) more times.

Place front loop

Next row: 1ch, 1sc into next 64 (69, 75, 80, 86) sc, 4ch, skip 4sc, 1sc into each sc to end, turn.

Next row: 1ch, 1sc into 1st sc, 1sc into next 63 (68, 74, 79, 85) sc, 4sc into 4ch sp, 1sc into each sc to end, turn.

Next row: 1ch, 1sc into 1st sc, 1sc into each sc to end, do not turn.

Work corded reverse sc trim along edge as follows With RS facing and using D/3 (3.00 mm) hook, start with the hook facing downwards; insert the hook from front to back into 1st st on the right hand side, *yo, draw the yarn back through towards yourself twisting the hook to face upwards, yo and draw through both loops on hook to complete the st, insert hook into next st to the right, rep from * to end.

Break off yarn and fasten off.

Button trim

With RS facing using G/6 (4.00 mm) hook and yarn A, insert hook at top edge of sc bodice and work 30 (30, 35, 35, 40) sc evenly down side edge of sc bodice, turn.

Row 2: 1ch, 1sc into each sc to end, turn.

Row 3: 1ch, 1sc into 1st 2sc, 3ch, * 1sc into next 5 (5, 6, 6, 7) sc, 3ch, rep from * to last 3sc, 1sc into each sc to end.

Break off yarn and fasten off.

Strap

Using D/3 (3.00 mm) hook, and yarn A make 155ch.

Row 1: 5ch, 1sc into 5th ch from hook, 1sc into each ch to end.

Break off yarn and fasten off.

to finish

Sew in all loose ends.
Block and press garment.
Sew buttons onto back, matching up with buttonhole loops.
Sew 2 buttons onto strap at opposite end from loop.
Place strap through loop in center front, fold in half and stitch together to secure.

sloppy joe beret

This design was inspired by all the gorgeous slouchy knitted hats that have graced the pages of fashion magazines over the past few autumn and winter seasons. The textured mock rib effect gives a quite bulky look that resembles a knitted fabric, which looks really chic.

star rating
★★☆ (intermediate)

finished size
To fit average adult ladies head

materials
- **Yarn:** Rowan Cocoon, 80% Merino wool 20% Kid Mohair (approx 126 yd/115 m per 3.5 oz/100 g ball) **3** Cloud, sh. 817 x 2 (blue)
- **Hook:** K/10½ (6.50 mm)

gauge
Using K/10½ (6.50 mm) hook approx 12sts and 11 rows over 4"/10 cm of textured pattern

abbreviations
Dc2tog – double crochet 2 together, dc2tog is worked in the back-post and front-post pattern
Fdc – Front-post double crochet
Bdc – Back-post double crochet
See also page 125

Using K/10½ (6.50 mm) hook make 5ch, sl st into 1st ch to make a ring.

Round 1: 2ch, 12dc into ring, sl st into top of 2ch at beginning of round. (12 sts)

Round 2: 2ch, (1Fdc, 1Bdc) into 1st dc, *(1Fdc, 1Bdc), into next dc, rep from * 10 more times, sl st into top of 2ch at beginning of round. (24 sts)

Round 3: 2ch, 1Fdc, (1Fdc, 1Bdc) into next dc, *1Fdc, (1Fdc, 1Bdc) into next dc, rep from * 10 more times, sl st into 2ch at beginning of round. (36 sts)

Round 4: 2ch, 1Fdc into 1st 2dc, (1Fdc, 1Bdc) into next dc,* 1Fdc into next 2dc, (1Fdc, 1Bdc) into next dc, rep from * 10 more times, sl st into top of 2ch at beginning of round. (48 sts)

Round 5: 2ch, 1Fdc into 1st 3dc, (1Fdc, 1Bdc) into next dc,* 1Fdc into next 2dc, (1Fdc, 1Bdc) into next dc, rep from * 10 more times, sl st into top of 2ch at beginning of round. (60 sts)

Round 6: 2ch, 1Fdc into 1st 4dc, (1Fdc, 1Bdc) into next dc,* 1Fdc into next 4dc, (1Fdc, 1Bdc) into next dc, rep from * 10 more times, sl st into top of 2ch at beginning of round. (72 sts)

Round 7: 2ch, 1Fdc into 1st 5dc, (1Fdc, 1Bdc) into next dc,* 1Fdc into next 5dc, (1Fdc, 1Bdc) into next dc, rep from * 10 more times, sl st into top of 2ch at beginning of round. (84 sts)

Round 8: 2ch, 1Fdc into 1st 6dc, (1Fdc, 1Bdc) into next dc,* 1Fdc into next 6dc, (1Fdc, 1Bdc) into next dc, rep from * 10 more times, sl st into top of 2ch at beginning of round. (96 sts)

Round 9: 2ch, 1Fdc into 1st 7dc, (1Fdc, 1Bdc) into next dc,* 1Fdc into next 7dc, (1Fdc, 1Bdc) into next dc, rep from * 10 more times, sl st into top of 2ch at beginning of round. (108 sts)

Round 10: 2ch, 1Fdc into 1st 8dc, 1Bdc into next dc, * 1Fdc into next 8dc, 1 Bdc into next dc, rep from * to end, sl st into top of 2ch at beg of round.

Round 11: As round 10.

Round 12: 2ch, *1Fdc into next 7sts, dc2tog as foll, yo, insert hook around front of next st, yo, and draw through, yo and draw under first 2 loops, yo, insert hook around back of next st, yo and draw through, yo and draw under first 2 loops, yo and draw under all loops on hook, rep from * 11 more times, sl st into 2ch at beg of round. (96 sts)

Round 13: 2ch, * 1Fdc into next 6dc, dc2tog as above over next 2dc, rep from * 11 more times, sl st into 2ch at beg of round. (84 sts)

Round 14: 2ch, * 1Fdc into next 5dc, dc2tog as above over next 2dc, rep from * 11 more times, sl st into 2ch at beg of round. (72 sts)

Round 15: 2ch, * 1Fdc into next 4dc, dc2tog as above over next 2dc, rep from * 11 more times, sl st into 2ch at beg of round. (60 sts)

Round 16: 2ch, * 1Fdc into next 3dc, dc2tog as above over next 2dc, rep from * 11 more times, sl st into 2ch at beg of round. (48sts)

Round 17: 2ch, * 1Fdc into next 2dc, dc2tog as above over next 2dc, rep from * 11 more times, sl st into 2 ch at beg of round. (36sts)

Round 19: 2ch, * 1Fdc into next 2dc, 1Bdc into next dc, rep from * 11 more times, sl st into 2ch at beg of round.

Repeat the last row if you want to make the band deeper.

Break off yarn and sew in any loose ends.

chunky chevron hooded scarf

Is it a scarf? Is it a hood? No, it's both! This two-in-one design will keep your head and neck snugly wrapped up from the winter chill. Worked in a merino wool and kid mohair chunky weight yarn it's super soft next to the skin. The chevron stitch will keep your interest as you work through the panels, and the corded trim adds the perfect finishing touch.

star rating

★ ★ ☆ (intermediate)

finished size

Actual measurements: width 10½ "/27 cm; length 52½ "/133 cm at hood

materials

- **Yarn:** Rowan Cocoon, 80% merino wool 20% kid mohair blend (approx 126 yd/ 115 m per 3.5 oz/100 g ball) Polar, sh. 801 x 5 (cream)
- **Hooks:** G/6 (4.00 mm) and J/10 (6.00 mm)

gauge

Using J/10 (6.00 mm) hook approx 12 sts and 6 rows over 4"/10 cm of double crochet

abbreviations

Fdc3tog – double crochet 3 together around front of stem
Fdc5tog – double crochet 5 together around front of stem
See also page 125

Left scarf panel

Using J/10 (6.00 mm) hook make 37ch.

Row 1: 1ch, 1sc into 2nd ch from hook, 1sc into each ch to end. (37 sts)

Row 2: 2ch, 1dc into 1st st, 3dc into next st, 1dc into next 14 sts, dc5tog over next 5 sts, 1dc into next 14 sts, 3dc into next st, 1dc into last st, turn.

Row 3–6: As row 2.

Row 7: 2ch, 1dc into 1st st, 2Fdc into next st, 1Fdc into next 14 sts, Fdc5tog over next 5 sts, 1Fdc into next 14 sts, 2Fdc into next st, 1dc into last st, turn. (35 sts)

Row 8: 2ch, 1dc into 1st st, 3dc into next st,1dc into next 13 sts, dc5tog over next 5 sts, 1dc into next 13 sts, 3dc into next st, 1dc into last st, turn.

Row 9–10: As last row.

Row 11: 2ch, 1dc into 1st st, 1Fdc into next 14 sts, Fdc5tog over next 5 sts, 1Fdc into next 14 sts, 1dc into last st, turn. (31sts)

Row 12: 2ch, 1dc into 1st st, 3dc into next st, 1dc into next 11 sts, dc5tog over next 5 sts, 1dc into next 11 sts, 3dc into next st, 1dc into last st, turn.

Row 13–14: As row 12.

Row 15: 2ch, 1dc into 1st st, 3Fdc into next st, 1Fdc into next 11 sts, Fdc5tog over next 5 sts, 1Fdc into next 11 sts, 3Fdc into next st, 1dc into last st, turn.

Row 16: 2ch, 1dc into 1st st, 3dc into next st, 1dc into next 11 sts, dc5tog over next 5 sts, 1dc into next 11 sts, 3dc into next st, 1dc into last st, turn.

Rows 17–18: As row 16.

Row 19: 2ch, 1dc into 1st st, 1Fdc into next 12 sts, 5Fdctog over next 5 sts, 1Fdc into next 12 sts, 1dc into last st, turn. (27 sts)

Row 20: 2ch, 1dc into 1st st, 3dc into next st, 1dc into next 9 sts, dc5tog over next 5 sts, 1dc into next 9 sts, 3dc into next st, 1dc into last st, turn.

Row 21–22: As row 20.

Row 23: 2ch, 1dc into 1st st, 3Fdc into next st, 1Fdc into next 9 sts, Fdc5tog over next 5 sts, 1Fdc into next 9 sts, 3Fdc into next st, 1dc into last st, turn.

Row 24–26: As row 20.

Row 27: As row 23.

Repeat rows 24–27, five more times.

Row 48: As row 23.

**Shape for hood by increasing on 1st half of chevron and keeping pattern correct on 2nd half, as follows:

Row 49 (inc): 2ch, 1dc into 1st st, 3dc into next st, 1dc into next 11 sts, dc3tog over next 3 sts, 1dc into next 9 sts, 3dc into next st, 1dc into last st. (29 sts)

Row 50: 2ch, 1dc into 1st st, 3dc into next st, 1dc into next 9 sts, dc3tog over next 3 sts, 1dc into each st to end, turn.

Row 51 (inc): 2ch, 1dc into 1st st, 3Fdc into next st, 1Fdc into next 13 sts, dc3tog over next 3 sts, 1Fdc into next 9 sts, 1 Fdc into next st, 1dc into last st, turn. (31sts)

Row 52: 2ch, 1dc into 1st st, 3dc into next st, 1dc into next 9 sts, dc3tog over next 3 sts, 1dc into each st to end, turn.

Row 53: 2ch, 1dc into each st to end, turn.

Row 54: As row 53.

Row 55: 2ch, 1dc into 1st st, 1Fdc into each st to end, turn.

Row 56: As row 53.

Repeat last 4 rows 3 more times then rows 53-54 once more.

Break off yarn and fasten off.

Right scarf panel

Work as given for left scarf panel until **

Shape for hood by keeping pattern correct on 1st half and increasing on 2nd half of chevron as follows:

Row 49 (inc): 2ch, 1dc into 1st st, 3dc into next st, 1dc into next 9 sts, dc3tog over next 3 sts, 1dc into next 11 sts, 3dc into next st, 1dc into last st. (29 sts)

Row 50: 2ch, 1dc into 1st st, 3dc into next st, 1dc into next 11 sts, dc3tog over next 3 sts, 1dc into each st to end, turn.

Row 51 (inc): 2ch, 1dc into 1st st, 3Fdc into next st, 1Fdc into next 9 sts, dc3tog over next 3 sts, 1Fdc into next 13 sts, 1 Fdc into next st, 1dc into last st, turn. (31 sts)

Row 52: 2ch, 1dc into 1st st, 3dc into next st, 1dc into next 15 sts, dc3tog over next 3 sts, 1dc into each st to end, turn.

Row 53: 2ch, 1dc into each st to end, turn.

Row 54: As row 53.

Row 55: 2ch, 1dc into 1st st, 1Fdc into each st to end, turn.

Row 56: As row 53.

Repeat last 4 rows 3 more times then rows 53-54 once more.

Break off yarn and fasten off.

to finish

Sew in all loose ends, block and press scarf and hood panels.

Using backstitch, sew top of hood panels together, then sew back seam of hood from start of head shaping. Work corded reverse sc trim around outer edge of scarf.

With RS facing and using G/6 (4.00 mm) hook rejoin yarn to center seam at the back of hood. Start with the hook facing downwards, insert the hook from front to back around the stem of the 1st st on the right hand side, *yarn round hook, draw the yarn back through towards yourself twisting the hook to face upwards, yo and draw through both loops on hook to complete the stitch, insert hook into next space to the right, rep from * to end around the outer edge of scarf and hood, sl st into first st.

Break off yarn and fasten off. Sew in loose ends.

girl's butterfly frill sleeve top

This is a sweet little design, which any little girl would love. It has pretty butterfly sleeves, but the colors make it not overly girly. The body is worked in a single crochet stitch, making the armhole shaping simple and easy to understand. The yarn is mercerized cotton, giving it a slight sheen that complements the powdery grey color of the body really well.

star rating
★★☆ (intermediate)

finished size
See chart page 126

materials
- **Yarn:** Rowan Cotton Glace, 100% cotton (approx 126 yd/115 m per 1.75 oz/50 g ball)
  A – Dawn grey, sh. 831 x 4, 5, 6
  B – Heather, sh. 828 x 2, 2, 3
  C – Chalk, sh 827 x 1 (sky blue)
- **Hook:** G/6 (4.00 mm)

gauge
Using G/6 (4.00 mm) hook approx 20 sts and 25 rows over 4"/10 cm of single crochet

abbreviations
Sc2tog – single crochet 2 together
Sc3tog – single crochet 3 together
See also page 125

Back

Using G/6 (4.00 mm) hook and yarn B make 61 (71, 81) ch.

Row 1 (RS): 1ch, 1sc into 2nd ch from hook, 1sc into each ch to end, turn. (61 (71, 81) sts)

Row 2: 1ch, 1sc into each sc to end, turn. Break off yarn B and change to yarn A.

Row 3: 1ch, 1sc into each sc to end, turn. Repeat row 3 until work measures 9½ (10¼, 11)"/24 (26, 28) cm, ending with RS facing for next row.

Shape for armholes

Row 1: Sl st across 1st 4 sts, 1ch, 1sc into next sc, 1sc into each sc to last 4 sc, turn. (53 (63, 73) sts)

Row 2: 1ch, 1sc into 2nd ch from hook, 1sc into each sc to end, turn.

Row 3: 1ch, 1sc into 1st sc, sc2tog, 1sc into each st to last 3sts, sc2tog, 1sc into last sc, turn. (51 (61, 71) sts)

Row 4: As row 3. (49 (59, 69) sts)

Row 5: 1ch, 1sc into 1st sc, 1sc into each st to end, turn.

Row 6: As row 3. (47 (57, 67) sts)

Rows 7–8: As row 5.

Row 9: As row 3. (45 (55, 65) sts)

Row 10: 1ch, 1sc into 1st st, 1sc into each st to end, turn. **

Repeat row 10 until armhole measures 6 (6¼, 6¾)"/15 (16, 17) cm, ending with RS facing for next row.

Shape shoulders

Next row: 1ch, 1sc into 1st st, 1sc into next 11 (13, 15) sts, turn. (12 (14, 16) sts)

Next row: 1ch, sl st into 1st 4 sts, 1ch, 1sc into each st to end, turn. (8 (10, 12) sts) Break off yarn and fasten off.

With RS facing, skip center 21 (27, 33) sts for back neck, rejoin yarn A in next st, 1ch, 1sc into same st, 1sc into each st to end, turn. (12 (14, 16) sts)

Next row: 1ch, 1sc into next 8 (10, 12) sts. Break off yarn and fasten off.

Front

Work as given for back until **.

Shape neck – work each side separately.

Row 11: 1ch, 1sc into 1st st, 1sc into next 11 (14, 17) sts, turn. (12 (15, 18) sts)

Work on these 12 (15,18) sts only.

Row 12-14: 1ch, 1sc into 1st st, 1sc into each st to end, turn.

Row 15: 1ch, 1sc into 1st st, 1sc into each st to last 3 sts, sc2tog, 1sc into last st, turn. (11 (14, 17) sts)

1st size

Repeat rows 12–15 3 more times. (8 sts)

2nd size

Repeat rows 12–15 4 more times. (10 sts)

3rd size

Repeat rows 12–15 5 more times. (12 sts)

All sizes

Keep working even until front armhole matches back to shoulder.

Break off yarn and fasten off.

With RS facing skip center 21 (25, 29) sts for front neck, rejoin yarn A in next st, 1ch, 1sc into same st, 1sc into each st to end, turn. (12 (15, 18) sts)

Work to match first side of neck, reversing shapings.

Break off yarn and fasten off.

to finish

Sew in all loose ends, then block and press front and back panels.
Sew shoulder seams together.

Neck trim
Using D/3 (3.00 mm) hook and with RS facing, rejoin yarn C to top left hand corner of neck.
Round 1: 1ch, 1sc into each sc down left hand side of front neck, place marker, work 1sc across front of neck, place marker, 1sc up right hand side of front neck, 1sc across back neck, sl st into 1ch at beg of round.
Round 2: 1ch, 1sc into each sc until 1st before marker, sc3tog over next 3 sts, 1sc into each st until 1 st before marker, sc3tog over next 3 sts, 1sc into each st to end, sl st into 1ch at beg of round.
Break off yarn C and join in yarn B.

Picot edge
Next round: 1ch, 1sl st into 1st 2 sts, 3ch, 1 sl st into next sc, * 1sl st into next 2 sts, 3ch, 1sl st into next sc, rep from * to end, sl st into 1ch at beg of round.
Break off yarn and fasten off.

Left armhole frill
Using G/6 (4.00 mm) hook and with RS facing join yarn B at front panel armhole.
Row 1: 1ch, work in sc evenly all round armhole, turn.
Row 2: 2ch, 2dc into each sc to end, turn.
Row 3: 3ch, 2tr into each dc to end, turn.
Row 4: 3ch, 1tr into each tr to end.
Break off yarn B and join in yarn C.
Work picot trim
Next row: 1ch, 1sl st into 1st 2 sts, 3ch, 1sl st into next st,*1sl st into next 2 sts, 3ch, 1sl st into next st, rep from * to end.
Break off yarn and fasten off.

Right armhole frill
Work as given for left hand frill start trim at front of armhole.
Sew side together.
Bottom picot trim edge, work as given for armhole trim.
Sew in all loose ends.

alpine hat

Keep your ears nice and cozy in winter with this cute earflap hat. The hat is worked in the round with broad stripes in shades of green from the top down. Each stitch is worked through the back loop of the stitch to add a little extra texture and interest to the fabric. The lambswool and kid mohair blend of fibers in the yarn also make the hat extra soft and snugly.

star rating
★★★ (intermediate)

finished size
Actual measurements 10½"/27 cm from top to earflap; width 22½"/57 cm

materials
- **Yarn:** Rowan Cocoon, chunky weight 80% merino and 20% kid mohair blend (approx 126 yd/115 m per 3.5 oz/100 g ball)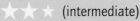
  A – Seascape, sh. 813 x 1 (Teal)
  B – Emerald, sh. 814 x 1
  C – Kiwi, sh. 816 x 1 (Lime)
- **Hook:** J/10 (6.00 mm)

gauge
Using J/10 (6.00 mm) hook approx 14 sts and 13 rows over 4"/10 cm of single crochet worked through back loop on the round

abbreviations
See page 125

Using a J/10 (6.00 mm) hook and yarn A make 4ch, sl st into 1st ch to make a ring.

Round 1: 1ch, 8sc into ring, sl st into top of 1ch at beginning of round. (8 sts)

Round 2: 1ch, 2sc into back loop of each sc to end, sl st into top of 1ch at beginning of round. (16 sts)

Round 3: 1ch, 1sc into back loop of each sc to end, sl st into top of 1ch at beginning of round. Break off yarn A and change to yarn B.

Round 4: As round 3.

Round 5: 1ch, 1sc into back loop of 1st sc, 2sc into back loop of next sc, * 1sc into back loop of next sc, 2sc into back loop of next sc, rep from * to end, sl st into top of ch at beginning of round. (24 sts)

Round 6: As round 3.

Break off yarn B and change to yarn C.

Round 7: As round 3.

Round 8: 1sc into back loop of 1st 2sc, 2sc into back loop of next sc, * 1sc into back loop of next 2sc, 2sc into back loop of next sc, rep from * to end, sl st into top of ch at beginning of round. (32 sts)

Round 9: As round 3.

Break off yarn C and change to yarn A.

Round 10: As round 3.

Round 11: 1sc into back loop of 1st 3sc, 2sc into back loop of next sc, * 1sc into back loop of next 3sc, 2sc into back loop of next sc, rep from * to end, sl st into top of ch at beginning of round. (40 sts)

Round 12: As round 3.

Break off yarn A and change to yarn B.

Round 13: 1sc into back loop of 1st 4sc, 2sc into back loop of next sc, * 1sc into back loop of next 4sc, 2sc into back loop of next sc, rep from * to end, sl st into top of ch at beginning of round. (48 sts)

Round 14: As round 3.

Round 15: 1sc into back loop of 1st 5sc, 2sc into back loop of next sc, * 1sc into back loop of next 5sc, 2sc into back loop of next sc, rep from * to end, sl st into top of ch at beginning of round. (56 sts)

Break off yarn B and change to yarn C.

Round 16: As round 3.

Round 17: 1sc into back loop of 1st 6sc, 2sc into back loop of next sc, * 1sc into back loop of next 6sc, 2sc into back loop of next sc, rep from * to end, sl st into top of ch at beginning of round. (64 sts)

Round 18: As round 3.

Break off yarn C and change to yarn A.

Round 19: 1sc into back loop of 1st 7sc, 2sc into back loop of next sc, * 1sc into back loop of next

7sc, 2sc into back loop of next sc, rep from * to end, sl st into top of ch at beginning of round. (72 sts)

Round 20: As round 3.

Round 21: 1sc into back loop of 1st 8sc, 2sc into back loop of next sc, * 1sc into back loop of next 8sc, 2sc into back loop of next sc, rep from * to end, sl st into top of ch at beg of round. (80 sts)

Break off yarn A and change to yarn B.

Round 22–24: As round 3.
Break off yarn B and change to yarn C.
Rounds 25–27: As round 3.
Break off yarn C and change to yarn A.
Start creating earflaps as follows, continuing to work into the back loop of each stitch.
Round 28: 1ch, 1sc into 1st st, 1sc into next 14 sts, 1hdc into next 2 sts, 1dc into next st, 1hdc into next 2 sts, 1sc into next 40 sts, 1hdc into next 2 sts, 1dc into next st, 1hdc into next 2 sts, 1sc into next 15 sts to end, sl st into top of ch at beg of round.
Round 29: 1ch, 1sc into 1st st, 1sc into next 13sts, 1hdc into next 2 sts, 1dc into next 3 sts, 1hdc into next 2 sts, 1sc into next 38 sts, 1hdc into next 2 sts, 1dc into next 3 sts, 1hdc into next 2 sts, 1sc into next 14 sts to end, sl st into top of ch at beg of round.
Round 30: 1ch, 1sc into 1st st, 1sc into next 12 sts, 1hdc into next 2 sts, 1dc into next 5 sts, 1hdc into next 2 sts, 1sc into next 36 sts, 1hdc into next 2 sts, 1dc into next 5 sts, 1hdc into next 2 sts, 1sc into next 13 sts to end, sl st into top of ch at beg of round.
Round 31: 1ch, 1sc into 1st st, 1sc into next 11 sts, 1hdc into next 2 sts, 1dc into next 7 sts, 1hdc into next 2 sts, 1sc into next 34 sts, 1hdc into next 2 sts, 1dc into next 7 sts, 1hdc into next 2 sts, 1sc into next 12 sts to end, sl st into top of ch at beg of round.
Round 32: 1ch, 1sc into 1st st, 1sc into next 10sts, 1hdc into next 2sts, 1dc into next 9sts, 1hdc into next 2sts, 1sc into next 32sts, 1hdc into next 2sts, 1dc into next 9sts, 1hdc into next 2sts, 1sc into next 11sts to end, sl st into top of ch at beginning of round.
Round 33: 1ch, 1sc into 1st st, 1sc into next 9sts, 1hdc into next 2 sts (place marker at 2nd hdc), 1dc into next 11 sts, 1hdc into next 2 sts, 1sc into next 30 sts, 1hdc into next 2 sts (place marker at 2nd hdc), 1dc into next 11 sts, 1hdc into next 2 sts, 1sc into next 10 sts to end, sl st into top of ch at beg of round.
Break off yarn and fasten off.

Earflaps

With RS facing, rejoin yarn at 1st marker (11th sts), sl st into 1st st, 1sc into next 3 sts, skip next 3 sts, 7dc into next st, skip 3 sts, 1sc into next 3 sts, 1sl st into next st, turn.

Next row: 1ch, skip 1st sl st, 1sc into next 4 sts, skip 2 sts, work 5dc into next st, skip 2 sts, 1sc into next 4 sts, skip 1 sts, sl st into next st.
Break off yarn and fasten off.
With RS facing, rejoin yarn at 2nd marker and complete second earflap as above.
Rejoin yarn B to center back seam.
Next row: 1ch, 1sc in each st to end, sl st into 1ch at beginning of round.
Break off yarn and fasten off.

Earflap ties

Cut 6 lengths of yarn B approx 23½"/60 cm long. Pull lengths through base of 5dc on last round of earflap. Make sure they are the same length at each side.
Split into 3 even sections and braid together. Tie a knot at the end to secure.

to finish

Sew in loose ends and press gently with a steam iron and damp cloth to ensure flaps lie flat.

jam jar covers

These shabby chic jam jar covers are a real blast from the past. But worked in brightly colored mercerized cotton and with pretty large glass beads around the edge, this retro classic is totally up to date. All you need now is the homemade jam to go with them.

star rating
★★☆ (intermediate)

finished size
Actual measurements:
   Diameter 4¾"/12 cm

materials
- **Yarn:** Rowan Siena, 4ply 100% mercerized cotton (approx 153 yd/140 m per 1.75 oz/50 g ball)
  A – Sloe, sh. 670 x 1 (purple)
  B – Beacon, sh. 667 x 1 (orange)
  C – Chilli, sh. 666 x 1 (red)
- Approx 12 glass beads per cover
- **Hook:** 5/6 (1.75 mm)

gauge
1 motif is 4¾"/12 cm wide

abbreviations
Dc4tog – double crochet 4 together
Dc5tog – double crochet 5 together
See also page 125

Thread beads on to yarn before starting.
Remember that the 1st bead you thread on will be the last bead you use.
Using 5/6 (1.75 mm) hook make 6ch, sl st into 1st ch to make a ring.

Round 1: 1ch, 12sc into ring, sl st into 1ch at beg of round.

Round 2: 1ch, 1sc into same place as 1ch, (7ch, skip 1sc, 1sc into next sc) 5 times, 3ch, skip 1sc, 1ddc into top of 1st sc.

Round 3: 3ch (counts as 1dc), 4dc into arch formed by ddc, (3ch, 5dc into next 7ch arch) 5 times, 3ch, sl st into top of 3ch at beg of round.

Round 4: 3ch (counts as 1dc), 1dc into each of next 4dc, *3ch, 1sc into next 3ch arch, 3ch **1dc into each of next 5dc, rep from * 4 more times and from * to ** again, sl st to top of 3ch at beg of round.

Round 5: 3ch, dc4tog over next 4dc (counts as dc5tog), * (5ch, 1sc into next 3ch arch) twice, 5ch **, dc5tog over next 5dc, rep from * 4 more times and from * to ** again, sl st to 1st cluster.

Round 6: Sl st into each of next 2ch, 1ch *1sc into next 5ch arch, 5ch, 5dc into next 5ch arch, 5ch, 1sc into 5ch arch, 5ch, rep from * to end, sl st into top of 1sc at beg or round.

Round 7: Sl st into each of next 2ch, 1ch, * 1sc into 5ch arch, 5ch, 1dc into next 5dc, (5ch, 1sc into next 5ch arch) twice, 5ch, rep from * to end, sl st into top of 1sc at beg of round.

Round 8: Sl st into each of next 2ch, 1ch, *1sc into 5ch arch, 5ch, bring bead up to hook bch, dc5tog (5ch, 1 sc into next 5ch arch) twice, 2ch, 1bch, 2ch, 1sc into next 5ch arch, 5ch, rep from * to end, sl st into top of 1sc at beg of round.
Break off yarn and fasten off.

to finish

Sew in loose ends.
Block and press to size.

cupcakes

These cute cupcakes are really good fun. Perfect as little gifts for friends and family, they use hardly any yarn and are ideal for using up all your scraps and leftovers. Play around with endless color combinations and sew some sequin and bead sprinkles on for an extra special effect.

star rating
★★ ☆ (intermediate)

finished size
Actual measurements: width 2¾"/7 cm; depth 2½"/6 cm

materials
- **Yarn:** Rowan Handknit Cotton, 100% cotton (approx 93 yd/85 m per 1.75 oz/ 50 g ball)
  A – Linen, sh. 205/Double choc, sh. 315 x 1
- Rowan Cotton Glace, 100% cotton (approx 126 yd/115 m per 1.75 oz/50 g ball)
  B – Bubbles, sh. 724 (pink)/Ecru, sh. 725 x1
  C – Poppy, sh. 741 x 1 (red)
- 100% DK organic cotton (approx 131 yd/120 m per 1.75 oz/50 g ball)
  D - Chlorophyll, sh. 992 (pale green)/ Madder, sh. 980 x 1 (peach)
- Toy stuffing
- **Hooks:** D/3 (3.00 mm) and 5/6 (1.75 mm)

gauge
Using D/3 (3.00 mm) hook and DK weight yarn approx 20 sts and 20 rows over 4"/10 cm of single crochet

abbreviations
See page 125

Pink icing cupcake

Base

Using D/3 (3.00 mm) hook and yarn A make 4ch, sl st into 1st ch to make a ring.

Round 1: 1ch, 8sc into ring, sl st into top of 1ch at beg of round. (8 sts)

Round 2: 1ch, 2sc into 1st sc, 2sc into each sc to end, sl st into top of 1ch at beg of round. (16 sts)

Round 3: 1ch, 1sc into 1st sc, 2sc into next sc, *1sc into next sc, 2sc into next sc, rep from * to end, sl st into top of 1ch at beg of round. (24 sts)

Side

Round 4: 8ch, work linked stitch as foll, insert hook into 2nd ch from hook, yo and draw through, (insert hook into next ch, yo and draw through) 6 times, insert hook into next sc yo and draw through – 9 loops on hook, (yo and draw through 2 loops) 8 times – 1 loop on hook, work 1 linked stitch inserting hook down through horizontal loop around stem of stitch instead of ch into each sc round outer edge of disc, close round by working sl st into top of 1st linked st.
Break off yarn and fasten off.

Icing

Using D/3 (3.00 mm) hook and yarn B make 4ch, sl st into 1st ch to make a ring.

Round 1: 1ch, 8sc into ring, sl st into top of 1ch at beg of round. (8 sts)

Round 2: 1ch, 2sc into 1st sc, 2sc into each sc to end, sl st into top of 1ch at beg of round. (16sts)

Round 3: 1ch, 1sc into 1st sc, 2sc into next sc, *1sc into next sc, 2sc into next sc, rep from * to end, sl st into top of 1ch at beg of round. (24 sts)

Round 4: 1ch, 1sc into 1st 2sc's, 2sc into next sc, *1sc into next 2sc, 2sc into next sc, rep from * to end, sl st into top of 1ch at beg of round. (32 sts)
Make icing drips as follows:

Round 5: 1ch, 1sc into 1st 3scs, 2sc into next sc, 1sc into next 3sc, 2sc into next sc, 1sc into next sc, 3ch, 1sc into next 2sc, 2sc into next sc, 1sc into next 3sc, 2sc into next sc, 1sc into next sc, 3ch, 1sc into next 2sc, 2sc into next sc, 1sc into next 3sc , 2sc into next sc, 1sc into next sc, 3ch, 1sc into next 2sc, 2sc into next sc, 1sc into next 3sc, 2sc into next sc, sl st into top of 1ch at beg of round.
Break off yarn and fasten off.

Cherry

Using 5/6 (1.75 mm) hook and yarn C make 4ch, sl st into 1st ch to make a ring.

Round 1: 1ch, 8sc into ring, sl st into top of 1ch at beg of round. (8 sts)

Round 2: 1ch, 2sc into 1st sc, 2sc into each sc to end, sl st into top of 1ch at beg of round. (16 sts)

Round 3: 1ch, 1sc into each sc to end, sl st into top of 1ch at beg of round.

Round 4: As round 3.

Round 5: 1ch, skip 1st sc, 1sc into next sc, * skip 1sc, 1sc into next sc, rep from * to end, sl st into top of 1ch at beg of round. (8 sts)

Green swirl cupcake

Base

Work as given for pink icing cupcake.

Icing

Use yarn D and work as given for pink icing cupcake.

Cherry

Work as given for pink icing cupcake.

Side

Using yarn A and D/3 (3.00 mm) hook make 10ch.

Row 1: 1ch, 1sc into each ch to end, turn. (10 sts)

Row 2: 1ch, 1sc into front loop of each sc to end, turn.

Row 3: 1ch, 1sc into back loop of each sc to end, turn.
Repeat rows 2–3, 9 more times.
Break off yarn and fasten off.

Icing swirl

Using D/3 (3.00 mm) hook and yarn D make 42ch.

Row 1: 1ch, 1sc into each ch to end, turn. (42 sts)

Row 2: 1ch, 1sc into each sc to end, turn.
Fold 2 row strip in half and join together to create tube by working a slip stitch along edge as follows:

Row 3: 1ch, insert hook into 1st sc and 1st ch, yo and draw through ch and sc. (2 loops on hook), draw 1st loop on hook under 2nd loop – 1 slip stitch worked, repeat this process through each sc and ch to end.
Break off yarn and fasten off.

to finish

Sew in all loose ends.

Pink icing cupcake

Sew cherry to center of icing. Insert toy stuffing into cupcake, make sure the base and sides are filled to the top, pin and stitch icing to top of sides, allow the picot icing drips to fall over the edge, leave a small gap to insert more stuffing if needed. Finish sewing icing to sides.

Green swirl cupcake

Sew top and bottom edges of side together. Sew one edge of side to base.

Coil up swirl and then pin and stitch to top of icing, sew cherry to top of swirl. Insert toy stuffing into cupcake, make sure the base and sides are filled to the top, pin and stitch icing to top of sides, allow the picot icing drips to fall over the edge, leave a small gap to insert more stuffing if needed. Finish sewing icing to sides.

white star throw

This light and airy throw is a modern classic and is the ultimate accessory for a chic, feminine space. The open lace motifs are worked in a DK weight cotton, which gives the star design real definition. Each motif is worked separately and joined together on the last round of the smaller motif, so no finishing is required. The throw can be any size you like by simply adding more motifs as you go.

star rating
★ ★ ★ (advanced)

finished size
Actual measurements: width 48"/122 cm; length 60"/153 cm

materials
- **Yarn:** Rowan Handknit Cotton, 100% cotton, (approx 93 yd/85 m per 1.75 oz/50 g ball) 3
  Ecru, sh. 251 x 20
  (add approx 1 ball for each extra large and small motif set)
- **Hook:** H/8 (5.00 mm)

gauge
1 large motif = 13½"/34 cm across

abbreviations
See page 125

Large Motif (make 20)

Using H/8 (5.00 mm) hook make 5ch, sl st into 1st ch to make a ring.

Round 1: 1ch, 10sc into ring, sl st into 1ch at beg of round. (10 sts)

Round 2: 1ch, 2sc into each sc to end, sl st into 1ch at beg of round. (20 sts)

Round 3: 4ch (counts as 1dc and 1ch), skip 1st sc, * 1dc into next sc, 1ch, rep from * to end, sl st into 3rd of 4ch at beg of round.

Round 4: 1ch, 1sc into same place as last sl st, * 6ch, 1sc into 2nd ch from hook, 1hdc into next ch, 1dc into next ch, 1tr into next ch, 1dtr into next ch, skip next 4sts (1ch, 1dc, 1ch, 1dc) and work 1sc into next ch, 6ch, 1sc into 2nd ch from hook, 1hdc into next ch, 1dc into next ch, 1tr into next ch, 1dtr into next ch, skip next 4sts (1dc, 1ch, 1dc, 1ch) and work 1sc into next dc, rep from * to end, replacing last sc with sl st into 1ch at beg of round. (8 triangles)

Round 5: Work 1sl st into each of the 5ch at base of first triangle, * 3ch, work 1sl st into top of sc, hdc and dc of dciangle, 5ch **, sl st into base of dc on next triangle, sl st into base of hdc and sc, rep from * 6 more times then from * to ** again, sl st into 3rd sl st worked at beg of round.

Round 6: Work 1sl st into each of the next 2sl st to top of triangle, 1ch, 1sc into 3ch at top of triangle, * 5ch, 3sc into next 5ch sp, 5ch, 1sc into 3ch at top of next triangle, rep from * replacing last sc with sl st into 1ch at beg of round.

Round 7: 1sl st into each of next 2ch, 1ch, 1sc into 5ch sp, * 5ch, 1sc into next 5ch sp, rep from * replacing last sc with sl st into 1ch at beg of round.

Round 8: 1sl st into each of next 2ch, 1ch, 3sc into 5ch sp,* 3ch, work (1dc, 3ch, 1tr, 3ch, 1tr, 3ch, 1dc) into next 5ch sp, 3ch, 3sc into next 5ch sp, rep from * to end, omitting 3sc at end of last rep, sl st into 1ch at beg of round.

Round 9: 1sl st into top of next 2sc, 4ch (counts as 1dc and 1ch), * 1hdc into next 3ch sp, 3ch, 1dc into next 3ch sp, 3ch, (1tr, 3ch, 1tr) into next 3ch sp, 3ch, 1dc into next 3ch sp, 3ch, 1hdc into next 3ch sp, 1ch, skip 1sc, 1dc into next sc, 1ch, rep from * to end, omitting 1dc and 1ch on last rep, sl st into 3rd of 4 ch at beg of round.

Round 10: 1ch, * 1sc into next 1ch sp, (1sc, 1hdc, 1dc, 1hdc, 1sc) into next 2 3ch sps, (1sc, 1hdc, 1dc, 1tr, 1dc, 1tr, 1sc) into next 3ch sp, (1sc, 1hdc, 1dc, 1hdc, 1sc) into next 2 3ch sps, 1sc into next 1ch sp, rep from * to end, sl st into 1ch at beg of round.

Break off yarn and fasten off.

Small motif (make 12)

Using H/8 (5.00 mm) hook make 4ch, sl st into 1st ch to make a ring.

Round 1: 6ch (counts as 1dc and 3ch), * 1dc into ring, 3ch, rep from * 6 times, sl st into 3rd of 6ch at beg of round.

Round 2: Sl st into 1st 2ch, 5ch, tr4tog into same sp as 2nd sl st, 5ch, skip (1ch, 1dc, 1ch), * tr5tog into 2nd ch of 3ch, 5ch, skip (1ch, 1dc, 1ch), rep from *6 more times, sl st into top of 1st cluster at beg of round.

Do not break off yarn, round 3 is worked when attaching motifs together.

Putting the motifs together

Round 3: Sl st into 1st 2ch of 5ch, 5ch, tr4tog into same place as 2nd sl st, insert hook from back to front through center dc of first small fan to the right hand side of large motif peak, and work 1sl st, sl st into each st until you reach center dc of 2nd fan, tr5tog (1 cluster) into 4th ch of same 5ch on small motif, sl st into next (hdc, 4sc, 1hdc and 1dc) of large motif, 1 cluster into 2nd ch of next 5ch on small motif, sl st into next (hdc, 2sc, hdc) on large motif, 1 cluster into 4th ch of same 5ch on small motif, sl st into next (hdc, 2sc, hdc, dc and tr) at top of motif peak , *3ch, sl st into tr at peak of 2nd large motif, now work 1sl st into next (dc, hdc, 2sc, hdc) of second motif, 1 cluster into 2nd ch of next 5ch on small motif, work 1sl st into next (dc, hdc, 2sc, hdc), work 1 cluster, 1sl st into next (dc, hdc, 2sc, hdc, dc and tr) at top of motif, rep from * joining 4 large motifs around outer edge of small motif.

Repeat round 3 until all small and large motifs are joined together. Use photograph as a guide.

Join outer edges together as follows:
You will be zig-zagging back and forth from the two large motifs.

Using H/8 (5.00 mm) hook, rejoin yarn to tr at center of 1st large motif peak at outer edge, 3ch, move across to next large motif and sl st into tr at

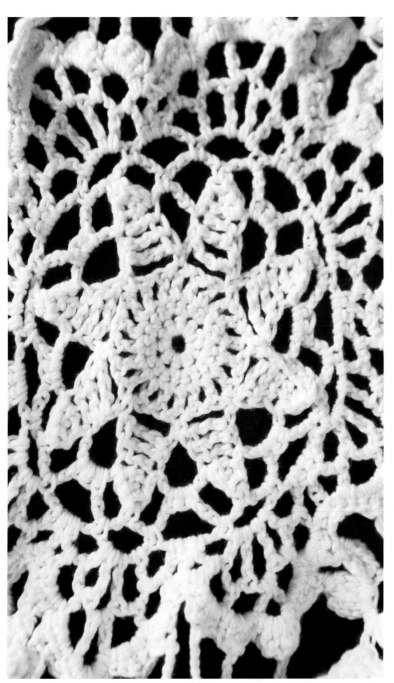

center of large motif peak, sl st into next (dc, hdc, 2sc, hdc, dc), 5ch, move back across to 1st motif and sl st into dc at center of 1st small fan, sl st into next (hdc, 2sc, hdc and dc), 7ch, move across to 2nd large motif, sl st into center dc of 2nd small fan, sl st into next (hdc, 4sc, hdc, dc), 7ch, move back across to 1st large motif, sl st into center dc of 3rd fan, sl st into next (hdc, 2sc, hdc), 5ch, move across to 2nd large motif and sl st into center dc of 4th fan, sl st into each st until you reach 3ch, sl st into base of 3ch.

Break off yarn and fasten off.

Repeat this process around outer edge.

Once all the small and large motifs are joined you will have spaces in between the large motifs – join together as follows using a similar method to the outer edge.

Using H/8 (5.00 mm) hook, rejoin yarn to center dc of 1st small fan, 5ch, move across to 2nd motif, sl st into center dc of 1st fan, sl st into next (hdc, 2sc, hdc and dc), 7ch, move back across to 1st motif, sl st into center dc of next fan, sl st into next (hdc, 4sc, hdc and dc), 7ch, move back across to 2nd motif, sl st into center dc of next fan, sl st into next (hdc, 2sc, hdc, dc), 5ch, move back across to 1st motif, sl st into center dc of next fan, sl st into each st until you reach 3ch, sl st into base of 3ch.

Break off yarn and fasten off.

Repeat this process until all gaps are filled.

Sew in all loose ends.

Block and press.

mock pleat shoulder bag

This bag looks more complicated than it actually is. The textured mock pleats are created using a linked stitch method, which is a good way of using longer stitches without the large gaps in between. The pretty coil petal flower adds a feminine touch and really complements the contrasting stripe pleats.

star rating
★★★ (advanced)

finished size
Actual measurements: base 16½"/42 cm; top 8½"/22 cm

materials
- **Yarn:** Rowan Calmer, DK weight, 75% cotton 75% acrylic micro fiber (approx 175 yd/160 m per 1.75 oz/50 g ball)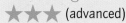
  A – Plum, sh. 493 x 3
  B – Garnet, sh. 492 x 1 (Red)
  C – Coral, sh. 476 x 1
- Flower – Rowan Siena, 4ply 100% mercerized cotton (approx 153 yd/140 m per 1.75 oz/50g ball)
  D – Rosette, sh. 664 x 1 (mid pink)
  E – Flounce, sh. 662 x 1 (bright pink)
  F – Chilli, sh. 666 x 1 (red)
  G – Lustre, sh. 665 x 1 (yellow)
- **Hooks:** G/6 (4.00 mm) and D/3 (3.00 mm)

gauge
Using G/6 (4.00 mm) hook approx 18 sts and 20 rows over 4"/10 cm of single crochet

abbreviations
Trltr – triple linked treble
See also page 125

Front and back (worked in one piece)
Using G/6 (4.00 mm) hook and yarn A make 36ch.

Row 1: 1ch, 1sc into 2nd ch from hook, 1sc into each ch to end, turn. (36 sts)

Row 2: 1ch, 1sc into 1st sc, 2sc into next sc, 1sc into each sc to last 2sts, 2sc into next sc, 1sc into last sc, turn. (38 sts)

Row 3–5: As row 2. (46 sts)

Row 6: 1ch, 1sc into 1st sc, 2sc into next sc, 1sc into each sc to last 2sc, 2sc into next sc, 1sc into last sc, make 11ch, turn.

Row 7: 1sc into 2nd ch from hook, 1sc into next 9ch, 1sc into next 46sc, make 11ch, turn.

Row 8: 1sc into 2nd ch from hook, 1sc into next 9ch, 1sc into next 56sc, make 11ch, turn.

Row 9: 1sc into 2nd ch from hook, 1sc into next 9ch, 1sc into next 66sc, make 11ch, turn.

Row 10: 1sc into 2nd ch from hook, 1sc into next 9ch, 1sc into next 76sc, turn. (86 sts)

Row 11: 1ch, 1sc into 1st st, 1sc into each st to end, turn.

Rows 12–13: As row 11.

Break off yarn A and join in yarn B.

Row 14: As row 11.

Work textured linked panel as follows:

Row 15: 5ch, work triple linked trebles (trltr) as follows: Starting 1st st by working into 5ch, insert hook into 2nd ch from hook, yo and draw through loop, (insert hook into next ch and draw through loop) 3 times, insert hook into next sc, yo and draw through loop – 6 loops on hook, (yo and draw under 1st 2 loops) 5 times – 1 loop on hook, 1st st is now complete. 1trltr as follows: Insert hook down through 1st horizontal loop of previous st, yo and draw through loop (insert hook down through next horizontal loop, yo and draw through loop) 3 times, insert hook into next sc, yo and draw through loop – 6 loops on hook, (yo and draw under 1st 2 loops) 5 times – 1 loop on hook, 2nd st is now complete. 1trltr into next 6sc, 1ch, insert hook into front loop at top of previous st, yo hook and draw through loop, work into remaining 4 horizontal loops of same st – 6 loops on hook, insert hook into base of st, yo and draw through loop – 7 loops on hook, insert hook into next sc, yo and draw through loop – 8 loops on hook, (yo and draw under 1st 2 loops) 7 times – 1 loop on hook, work next 16 sts using same linked method as st just made, 1ch, insert hook into 1st loop of previous st, yo hook and draw through loop, work into remaining 5 horizontal loops of same st – 7 loops on hook, insert hook into base of st, yo and draw through loop – 8 loops on hook, insert hook into next sc, yo and draw through loop – 9 loops on hook, (yo and draw under 1st 2 loops) 8 times – 1 loop on hook, work next 35 sts using linked method as st just made.

Make next st as follows: Skip 1st loop of last st made, work linked method into next 5 loops of stitch, skip last loop, insert hook into next sc, yo and draw through loop – 7 loops on hook (yo and draw under 1st 2 loops) 6 times – 1 loop on hook, work linked method with 7 loops on next 16sts.

Make next st as follows: Skip 1st loop of last st made, work linked method into next 3 loops of stitch, skip last loop, insert hook into next sc, yo and draw through loop – 5 loops on hook (yo and draw under 1st 2 loops) 4 times – 1 loop on hook, work linked method with 5 loops on remaining 7 sts, turn. Complete mock pleat by working into matching sc at other side of textured linked st panel as follows:

Row 16: 1ch, * insert hook from right to left around stem of sc at base on next st then insert hook into top of same st, yo and draw through loop, yo and draw through 2 loops on hook **, rep from * to ** 24 more times, 1sc into next 36 sts, rep from * to **25 times, turn.

Break off yarn B and join in yarn A.

Row 17–25: 1ch, 1sc into 1st st, 1sc into each st to end, turn.

Break off yarn A and join in yarn C.

Rows 26–35: As rows 14–25.

Repeat rows 14–32 once more.

Next row: Sl st across 1st 10sts, 1ch, 1sc into next 66 sts, turn. (66 sts)

Next row: Sl st across 1st 10sts, 1ch, 1sc into next 46sts, turn. (46 sts)

Next row: 1ch, 1sc into 1st st, sc2tog, 1sc into each st to last 3 sts, sc2tog, 1sc into last st, turn. (44 sts)

Repeat last row 4 more times. (36 sts).

Next row: 1ch, 1sc into 1st st, 1sc into each st to end.

Break off yarn and fasten off.

Bag top (make 2)
Using G/6 (4.00 mm) hook and yarn A make 40ch.
Row 1: 1ch, 1sc into 1st ch, 1sc into each ch to end, turn. (40 sts)
Row 2: 1ch, 1sc into 1st st, 1sc into each st to end, turn.
Rows 3–10: As row 2.
Row 11: 1ch, 1sc into back loop of 1st sc, 1sc into back loop of each sc to end, turn.
Rows 12–20: As row 2.
Break off yarn and fasten off.

Handles (make 2)
Using yarn A and G/6 (4.00 mm) hook make 80ch.
Row 1: 5ch, work 1trltr as described on row 15 of bag into 1st ch, 1trltr into each ch to end.
Break off yarn and fasten off.

to finish

Sew in all loose ends, block and press all pieces.
Fold bag top in half, pin into place along top opening – use picture as guide, allow approx 1"/2.5 cm of main body of bag to be sandwiched in between front of back of top trim, stitch into place using backstitch.
Fold main body of bag in half and sew side seams from base to bottom of bag top, leave this open.

Handles
Fold in half with RS to the outside and sew sides together length wise to form tube.
Pin one handle to outer edge of bag, approx above first and last textured color section, sew to bag using backstitch.
Repeat process for other side of bag.

Coil flower
Using D/3 (3.00 mm) hook and yarn D make 6ch, sl st into 1st ch to make a ring.
Round 1: 1ch, 12sc into ring, sl st into 1ch at beg of round.
Break off yarn D and join in yarn E.
Round 2: * work 1 coil of (12ch, 5dc into 4th ch from hook, 5dc into each of next 8ch, sl st into same place as 12ch), 1sl st into each of next 2sc, rep from * 5 more times, omitting 1sl st at end of last rep.
Break off yarn and fasten off.
Sew in loose ends.
Thread embroidery needle with yarn F. Work 8 French knots at center of flower, then thread embroidery needle with yarn G. Using picture as guide, bring needle up through contrast center from back to front and down through center ring, almost wrapping yarn around in between the French knots.
Sew flower to front of bag, using photograph as a guide.

deep v skinny tunic

This nautical feel tunic is worked throughout in a combination of basic stitches, which gives the fabric a slightly textured appearance. It is worked in a larger hook than would normally be used for a DK weight, while the silk and merino mix yarn gives the fabric bulk without the weight. The bold contrasting stripe is balanced by the solid broad trim at the armhole, but this design would look just as good worked in a solid color.

star rating
★★★ (advanced)

finished size
See chart page 126

materials
- **Yarn:** Rowan Silk Wool DK, 50% silk, 50% merino wool (approx 109 yd/100 m per 1.75 oz/50g ball)
  A – Lip gloss, sh. 312 x 6, 7, 7, 8 (red)
  B – Milk, sh. 300 x 5, 5, 6, 6 (ecru)
- **Hook:** H/8 (5.00 mm)

gauge
Using H/8 (5.00 mm) hook 5 repeats and 12 rows over 4"/10 cm of pattern

abbreviations
Sc2tog – single crochet 2 together
Hdc2tog – work two half double crochets together as follows: * yo insert hook into next st, yo and pull through, rep from * twice, (5 loops on hook), yo and draw through all loops on hook
See also page 125

Back

Using H/8 (5.00 mm) hook and yarn A make 63 (69, 75, 81, 87) ch.

Row 1: 1ch, 1sc into 2nd ch from hook, 1sc into each ch to end, turn. (63 (69, 75, 81, 87) sts)

Row 2: 2ch, (1hdc, 1dc) into 1st sc, * skip 2 sts, (1sc, 1hdc, 1dc) into next st, rep from * to last 2 sts, skip 2sc, 1sc into tch, turn. (21 (23, 25, 27, 29) pattern repeats)

Rows 3-7: As row 2.

Break off yarn A and join in yarn B.

Rows 8-13: As row 2.

Break off yarn B and join in yarn A.

Rows 14-19: As row 2.

Break off yarn A join in yarn B.

Row 20 (dec): 2ch, skip 1st sc, hdc2tog over next 2 sts, (1sc, 1hdc, 1dc) into next sc, skip 2sts, * (1sc, 1hdc, 1dc) into next st, skip 2 sts, rep from * to last 2 sts, skip 2 sts, 1sc into tch, turn.

Row 21(dec): 2ch, skip 1st sc, hdc2tog over next 2 sts, (1sc, 1hdc, 1dc) into next st, skip 2 sts, *(1sc, 1hdc, 1dc) into next st, skip 2 sts, rep from * to last 2sts, hdc2tog, 1sc into tch, turn.

Row 22: 2ch, (1hdc, 1dc) into 1st sc, skip 2 sts, *(1sc, 1hdc, 1dc) into next st, skip 2 sts, rep from * to last 2sts, hdc2tog, 1sc into tch, turn. 19 (21, 23, 25, 27) pattern repeats)

Rows 23-26: As row 2.

Break off yarn B and join in yarn A.

Rows 27-32: As row 2.

Break off yarn A and join in yarn B.

Rows 33-38: As row 2.

Rows 27-38: Form 12 row stripe pattern.

1st and 2nd sizes

Repeat rows 27-38 stripe 3 more times, then row 27-28 once more.

3rd and 4th sizes

Repeat rows 27-38 stripe 3 more times, then row 27-28 twice more.

5th size

Repeat rows 27-38 stripe 3 more times, then row 27-32 once more.

All sizes

Break off yarn and fasten off.

Front

Work as given for back until work measures approx 15½ (16, 17, 17¾, 18½) in/39 (41, 43, 45, 47) cm, ending on a WS row and working 12 row stripe pattern throughout.

Shape neck

Row 1 (RS): 2ch, (1hdc, 1dc) into 1st sc, * skip 2 sts (1sc, 1hdc, 1dc) into next sc, rep from * 6 (7, 8, 9, 10) times more, 1sc into next st, 1hdc into next 2 sts, turn. (9 (10, 11, 12, 13) repeats)

Row 2: 2ch, 1hdc into next 2 sts, (1sc, 1hdc, 1dc) into next st, * skip 2 sts, (1sc, 1hdc, 1dc) into next st, rep from * to last 2 sts, skip 2 sts, 1sc into tch, turn.

Row 3: 2ch, (1hdc, 1dc) into 1st sc, * skip 2sts, (1sc, 1hdc, 1dc) into next sc, rep from * to last 7 sts, skip 2 sts, 1sc into next st, 1hdc into next 5 sts, turn.

Row 4: 2ch, 1hdc into next 2 sts, hdc2tog over next 2 sts, 1sc into next st, (1sc, 1hdc, 1dc) into next st, * skip 2 sts, (1sc, 1hdc, 1dc) into next st, rep from * to last 2 sts, skip 2 sts, 1sc into tch, turn.

Row 5: 2ch, (1hdc, 1dc) into 1st sc, * skip 2 sts, (1sc, 1hdc, 1dc) into next sc, rep from * to last 4 sts, hdc2tog over next 2 sts, 1hdc into next 2 sts, turn.

Row 6: 2ch, 1hdc into next 2sts, sc2tog over next 2sts, (1hdc, 1dc) into same place as 2nd stitch of the sc2tog, *skip 2sts, (1sc, 1hdc, 1dc) into next sc, rep from * to last 2sts, 1sc into tch, turn (8, 9, 10, 11, 12) repeats.

Row 7: 2ch, (1hdc, 1dc) into 1st sc, * skip 2sts, (1sc, 1hdc, 1dc) into next sc, rep from * until 3sts, 1sc into next st, 1hdc into next 2sts, turn.

Row 8: As row 2.

Row 9: As row 3.

Row 10: As row 4.

Row 11: As row 5.

Row 12: As row 6.

Keeping stripe pattern as set, repeat rows 7-12 until 5 (5, 7, 8, 8) pattern repeats have been worked, ending on a WS row.

Next row: As row 7.

Next row: As row 8.

Repeat last 2 rows until front matches back for length.

Rejoin yarn to start of neck shaping and reverse shaping to match left hand side.

to finish

Block and press front and back of garment. Sew shoulder seams together.

Neck trim

With RS facing, using yarn A and H/8 (5.00 mm) hook, rejoin yarn to top left hand shoulder seam.
Round 1: 1ch, work 38 (38, 40, 42, 44) sc down left hand side of front neck, 1sc into center point, place marker and 38 (38, 40, 42, 44) sc up right hand side of front neck, then 22 (24, 22, 22, 24) sc along back neck, sl st into 1ch at beg of row. (99 (101, 103 107, 113) sts)
Round 2: 1ch, 1sc into each sc until 1sc before marker, sc3tog over next 3sc, 1sc into each sc to end, sl st into 1ch at beg of round. (97 (99, 101, 105, 110) sts)
Break off yarn and fasten off.

Left sleeve trim

With RS of front facing, using yarn A and H/8 (5.00 mm) hook rejoin yarn 6 stripes up from bottom.
Row 1: 1ch, work 46 (46, 48, 48, 50) sc up to shoulder seam, then 46 (46, 48, 48, 50) sc's down to same point on back, turn. (92 (92, 96, 96, 100) sts)
Row 2: 1ch, 1sc into each sc to end, turn.
Row 3: 1ch, 1sc into 1st sc, sc2tog over next 2 sts, 1sc into next 40 (40, 42, 42, 44) sts, sc2tog over next 2 sts, 1sc into next 2 sts, sc2tog over next 2 sts, 1sc into each st to last 3 sts, sc2tog over next 2 sts, 1sc into last st, turn. (88 (88, 92, 92, 94) sts)
Row 4: 1ch, 1sc into 1st sc, sc2tog over next 2 sts, 1sc into each st to last 3 sts, sc2tog over next 2 sts, 1sc into last st, turn. (86 (86, 90, 90, 94) sts)
Row 5: As row 4. (84 (84, 88, 88, 92) sts)
Row 6–8: As row 2.
Row 9: 1ch, 1sc into next 39 (39, 41, 41, 43) sts, sc2tog over next 2sts, 1sc into next 2sts, sc2tog over next 2sts, 1sc into each st to end, turn. (82 (82, 86, 86, 90) sts)
Row 10–12: As row 2.
Break off yarn and fasten off.

Right sleeve trim

Work as given for left sleeve trim, rejoining yarn at back. Sew in all loose ends. Sew up side seams and sleeve trim seams.

Crochet hook conversion chart

Metric	USA	Old UK
1.75 mm	5 or 6	15 or 2½ or 3
2.00 mm	B/1	14 or 1½ or 1
2.50 mm	C/2	12 or 0 or 2/0
3.00 mm	D/3	10 or 11 or 3/0
3.50 mm	E/4	9
4.00 mm	F/5	8
4.50 mm	G/6	7
5.00 mm	H/8	6
5.50 mm	I/9	5
6.00 mm	J/10	4
6.50 mm	K/10½	3
7.00 mm	No equivalent	2
7.50 mm	No equivalent	1
8.00 mm	L/11	0
9.00 mm	M/13	00
10.00 mm	N/15	000
12.00 mm	O/16	No equivalent

Table of abbreviations

Bdc – back post double crochet

Ch – chain

Ch sp – chain space

Dc – double crochet

Dc2tog – double crochet 2 together

Dc3tog – double crochet 3 together

Dc4tog – double crochet 4 together

Dc5tog – double crochet 5 together

Dltr –double linked treble

Exdc – extended dc

Fdc – front post double crochet

Fdc3tog – double crochet 3 together around front of stem

Fdc5tog – double crochet 5 together around front of stem

Hdc – half double crochet

Hdc2tog – half double crochet 2 together

Ldc – linked double crochet

Ltr – linked treble

Sc – single crochet

Sc2tog – single crochet 2 together

Sl st – slip stitch

Tr – treble

Trltr – triple linked treble

Tch – turning chain

Tog - together

TP – triple picot

Yo – yarn over

Finished size chart

For adults

To fit bust:	inches	32	34	36	38	40
	cm	81	86	91	96	101
Actual size	inches	34	36	38	40	42
	cm	86	91	96	101	106
Length	inches	25.5	27	28	29	30.5
	cm	65	68	71	74	77

For children

To fit: Chest size:		3-4 yrs	4-5 yrs	6-7 yrs
	inches	23	24	26
	cm	58	61	66
Actual size	inches	24	26	28
	cm	61	66	71
Length	inches	11.5	12.5	13.75
	cm	29	32	35

Yarn Weight Symbol & Category Names	0 lace	1 super fine	2 fine	3 light	4 medium	5 bulky	6 super bulky
Type of Yarns in Category	Fingering 10-count crochet thread	Sock, Fingering, Baby	Sport, Baby	DK, Light Worsted	Worsted, Afghan, Aran	Chunky, Craft, Rug	Bulky, Roving

Source: Craft Yarn Council of America's www.YarnStandards.com

Index

Acknowledgments

A huge thanks to my other half Andy Daly and great friend Jane Galbraith, who's encouragement, support and helping hands made everything possible. I would also like to thank Kate Buller and the team at Rowan for sponsoring me and providing all the gorgeous yarns.